PASSAGES ON THE CRIMEAN WAR

The Journal of Private Richard Barnham
38th Regiment, South Staffordshire

Foreword by David Cliff
Founder & Vice-President of the Crimean War Research Society

Lundarien Press

First Published by Lundarien Press, UK, 2015
Introduction Copyright © Phin Hall 2015
Foreword Copyright © David Cliff 2015

ISBN 978-1-910816-78-3

To the memory of
Marion Russell, who always wanted to see her
great-grandfather's diary in print

CONTENTS

INTRODUCTION by Phin Hall

Richard William Barnham was born on 2 August 1832. One hundred and fifty-five years later, my grandmother, Marion Russell, gave me a typed-up copy of his Crimean War journal. I was only 11 years old at the time, and not especially excited at receiving this document, despite the fact the author was my great-great-great grandfather. After all, they were just a load of pages full of words, without a single picture among them. My grandma's hope was that I would eventually do something with this journal, but at the time I had no idea what this might be. Instead, I hid the journal away in the attic.

Eighteen years later, having been involved in independent book publishing for a few years, I suddenly remembered those old photocopied pages and, on an impulse, crawled around among the dusty cobwebs and relics of my childhood until I found them tucked away beneath a stack of old newspapers and badly written poems. And so began the journey that has led to this publication.

My grandma had said she believed the original, hand-written journal was destroyed back when the Leeds Rifles Museum had shut down. Thinking, then, that the pages from my loft were all that remained, I carefully typed them up on my computer in preparation for publication.

In an attempt to find out a little more about Richard Barnham, I contacted the Staffordshire Regiment Museum (the 38th Staffordshire Regiment of Foot having been amalgamated into the South Staffordshire Regiment in 1881) in Litchfield and was amazed at the vast amount of material that was sent to me by Jeff Elson, the Head of

Research there. Not only did this include a copy of the very pages I had received in 1987, but there was also a letter written by Richard to his parents (see Appendix 1), a photograph of him, and a few photographs of the original journal itself. At first I naturally assumed the museum had only these photographs, but Mr Elson informed me that he had taken them himself when I sent through the request - they had the journal! Fast-forward a couple of months and I spent a wonderful, sunny morning sitting in the museum's reading room, going through the original journal, photographing each page as I did so. Some of these I have included in the appendices, but the remainder can be found on the Lundarien Press website.

Having the original, handwritten document proved invaluable as there were a number of passages in the typed copy that did not make sense and it turned out that some lines had been skipped and, in a couple of places, whole sections had been overlooked. These have now been added back in.

That said, not *everything* made sense or flowed properly, since Richard wrote the journal whilst on campaign - my understanding is that it was first scribbled down as notes while in the Crimea, then written up in the journal when his regiment was posted to Ireland. I have made as few changes as possible to the original text, but where necessary I have amended grammar ("we was" being a favourite of Richard's), deleted redundant repetitions, altered phrases that didn't make sense and, where known, corrected the spelling of place names. As mentioned above, though, the original, handwritten version can be viewed on the Lundarien Press website.

So what about Richard Barnham himself? There is not a vast amount of information to be gleaned about him, but what there is tells us that he was born in Norwich, Norfolk to Richard and Mary Barnham, and was baptised a few days later. At the age of 18, in February 1851, he enlisted with the 38th Regiment - corporal (private) 3041. He was 22 years old when the Crimean War began and took part in the battles of Alma, Inkerman and the Siege of Sebastopol, receiving a medal with these three clasps.

While that appears to have been Richard's first taste of action, it wasn't the last as, shortly afterwards, he was sent with the regiment to fight in the Indian Mutiny of 1857, receiving another medal, this time with the clasp of Lucknow.

Crimean Medal as received by Richard Barnham

Ten years after enlisting, in December 1861, he was discharged in Colchester after which time he moved to Leeds, where he was employed as a Sergeant Instructor by the Leeds Rifles. On 18 March 1862, he married Bessy Burton at St Giles parish church in Pontefract, Yorkshire.

At some point soon after, Richard left the Leeds Rifles. In an 1872 newspaper article, he is mentioned as the steward of the new Leeds Billiards Club, and in the1881 census, aged 49, he is listed as a wharfinger, managing a quay on the Leeds and Liverpool Canal. In amongst all this work, Richard and Bessy managed to have at least ten children, the oldest of whom, William Arthur Barnham, was my great-great grandfather.

On 29 September 1919, aged 87, Richard Barnham died, having just lived through yet another war, and was buried in Leeds' Holbeck Cemetery. The notice in the Yorkshire Evening Post read:

> *"The Victorian Veterans Society - all members of the above society are requested to attend the funeral of the late Sergeant Instructor Richard Barnham, Crimean and Indian Mutiny veteran. Meet at 14 Rawson Terrace, Friday Oct 3rd at 2.30."*

Shortly before publishing this book, I was given some additional information on Richard Barnham written by my grandma, Marion Russell, who was born during Richard's lifetime, and I have included this in the appendices.

I am no expert on the Crimean War. Thankfully, many who are have written books and articles on the subject and, while going through Richard's journal, I consulted some of these to check what he had written against the official records. I have listed a few of these works in the Further Reading section at the end of this book, and the foreword by David Cliff, which follows this introduction, provides an excellent overview of the politics behind the war, the various battles it included and the numbers of those involved.

I will not attempt to replicate the work carried out by other, far more scholarly and well-informed people, but I have what follows is a brief overview of the Crimean War (focusing on the events that affected Richard Barnham) that may help before getting into the journal itself:

- <u>5 Oct 1853</u>: Turkey declares war on Russia
- <u>28 Mar 1854</u>: France and Great Britain declare war on Russia
- <u>5 Apr</u>: First British troops arrive at Gallipoli
- <u>27 Apr</u>: 38th Regiment, including Richard Barnham, departs from Portsmouth
- <u>17 May</u>: 38th Regiment arrives at Gallipoli
- <u>22 Jun</u>: 38th Regiment departs for Varna, arriving 26 June
- <u>10 Aug</u>: Fire destroys much of the commissariat stores
- <u>3 Sep</u>: Allies set out from Varna for the Crimea
- <u>14 Sep</u>: Landing at Calamita Bay
- <u>20 Sep</u>: Battle of Alma
- <u>25 Sep</u>: British troops march past McKenzie's Farm en route to Sebastopol
- <u>27 Sep</u>: British arrive at Balaclava
- <u>17 Oct</u>: Siege of Sebastopol begins with the first bombardment
- <u>25 Oct</u>: Battle of Balaclava (Richard Barnham records this, but was not there)
- <u>5 Nov</u>: Battle of Inkerman (also Florence Nightingale arrives at the Scutari hospital)
- <u>14 Nov</u>: Hurricane devastates the Crimea
- <u>9 Apr 1855</u>: Second 'bombardment' of Sebastopol
- <u>6 Jun</u>: Third 'bombardment' of Sebastopol
- <u>8-9 Jun</u>: Allies capture the Mamelon and the Quarries
- <u>17 Jun</u>: Fourth 'bombardment' of Sebastopol

- <u>18 Jun</u>: Allied assault on Malakoff and Redan is repelled
- <u>28 Jun</u>: Death of Lord Raglan
- <u>17 Aug</u>: Fifth 'bombardment' of Sebastopol
- <u>5 Sep</u>: Sixth 'bombardment' of Sebastopol
- <u>8 Sep</u>: French seize Malakoff, British fail to take the Redan
- <u>9 Sep</u>: Russians evacuate Sebastopol
- <u>15 Nov</u>: French magazine at Sebastopol explodes
- <u>30 Mar 1856</u>: The Treaty of Paris is signed *(war formally ends 27 April)*
- <u>26 Jun</u>: 38th Regiment departs for England

Phin Hall with Richard Barnham's journal

FOREWORD by David Cliff

The Crimean War, originally called 'The Eastern War' or 'The Russian War', began when Turkey, supported by Britain and France, refused to accede to certain demands made by Russia. This led to a Russian invasion of Moldavia and Wallachia, the northern provinces of the Turkish Empire. Britain and France were fearful that Russia would overrun the declining Turkish Empire ('The Sick Man of Europe') and gain control of the Bosphorus and the Dardanelles. This would allow Russian warships from Sevastopol, the main Russian naval base in the Black Sea, a passage into the Mediterranean. The British and French sent warships to support the Turks, but following the 'massacre' of 4,000 Turkish sailors at Sinope on 30 November 1853, they resolved to send armies to give further support to the Turks. A formal treaty of alliance was signed by Britain and France on 10 April 1854, and by Turkey five days later.

The allied armies first landed at Varna on the Black Sea coast of Turkey and marched inland where they set up their camps. The aim was to support the Turks, who were holding the line of the River Danube against the Russian invaders. As described by Barnham, the deadly disease of Cholera soon appeared amongst the allied armies and thinned out their ranks considerably.

Incredibly, on 26 June 1854, the Russians lifted the siege of the Turkish fortress of Silistria and began to retire northwards, and by 2 August they had withdrawn completely from Turkish territory.

Political and public opinion in London and Paris would not allow the troops to return home without a fight, and

Lord Raglan, the commander of the British Army of the East, was given orders, in conjunction with the French, to attack and destroy the Russian naval base of Sevastopol in the Crimea, along with the Russian fleet anchored there.

Numerous accounts of the war were afterwards written by British officers who took part, but accounts by the rank and file are relatively rare and this memoir written by Barnham, a serving Private (later Corporal), is to be welcomed. Written in an educated hand, it informs us of what it was like to 'live rough' on campaign, and the struggle to keep warm and dry and to find enough to eat and drink. This was in addition to the dangers faced on the battlefield and in the trenches in front of Sevastopol. The account adds greatly to our knowledge and understanding of the war.

Barnham at times gives several statistics regarding the numbers of troops involved in various battles and actions and the casualties suffered; no doubt this is largely based on the camp gossip and rumour of the time.

He states that the Russians attacked at Balaclava with 50,000 men when a more accurate estimate would be half that number, also that they lost 'thousands' of men in the battle when a more realistic figure would be 240 killed and just over 300 badly wounded. As a result of the infamous Charge of the Light Brigade, he states that only 200 returned, this is correct if he is referring to those who returned still mounted. The strength of the Light Brigade before going into action is now generally accepted to be around 673, of those 113 men were killed and 247 badly wounded; in addition 475 horse were lost.

He again over-estimates the number of Russians who

took part in the battle of Inkerman, the true figure being just over 40,000 compared to his figure of 60,000 to 80,000. He does however under-estimate the number of British troops at 6,000 when 7,500 is a more accurate figure. His figure for the Russian casualties (20,000) is about double what they actually were, while the British and French suffered in the region of 3,300 killed and wounded, not 6,000.

Barnham was a Private (later Corporal) in the 38th (The 1st Staffordshire) Regiment of Foot and includes in his account some details regarding the casualties suffered by the regiment during the campaign; these are essentially correct. The regiment started the war over 900 strong and, even by the time of the landing in the Crimea, it had been reduced to 714, mainly due to diseases, especially cholera. The harsh winter of 1854-55 decimated the British Army, who lived in tents while serving in the trenches before Sevastopol. He states that by April 1855 there were only 350 effectives left in the regiment; I have no reason to doubt this figure. Having returned to England, the regiment was reviewed by Queen Victoria on 12 August 1856 and, as Barnham states, there were only 130 men present who went to the East at the beginning of the war.

His figure of 350 men of the 38th killed and wounded during the first attack on the Redan bastion on 18 June 1855 is however on the high side, 'only' 150 being listed in the casualty lists. On the same day the French attacked the Malakoff fortress and suffered 3,500 casualties, 500 less than stated by Barnham.

The Allies again attacked the Russian defences on 8 September 1855 and, while the British failed to capture the Redan, the French took the Malakoff, resulting in the

Russians abandoning the south side of Sevastopol. The dockyard facilities and military installations were then systematically destroyed by the allies. Early in 1856 an armistice was agreed and peace negotiations commenced in Paris. The Treaty of Peace was signed on 30 March 1856.

The war had little lasting effect; Russia repudiated the treaty in 1870 while France was at war with Prussia. In 1876 Russia and Turkey were again fighting each other, but this time Britain and France stayed out of the conflict. Sevastopol recovered and again became the most important Russian naval base in the Black Sea. In 1991, with the break-up of the Soviet Union, Ukraine including the Crimea became an independent nation. By agreement the naval base of Sevastopol was shared by the Ukraine and Russian navies. However, recently, as the result of Ukraine aligning herself with the West, Russia has again re-occupied the Crimea.

David Cliff, Founder & Vice-President of the Crimean War Research Society
July 2015

PASSAGES ON THE CRIMEAN WAR

Richard Barnham

1. VOYAGE TO GALLIPOLI: APRIL - JUNE 1854

The 38th Regiment left the shores of old England at Portsmouth on the 27th day of April in the year of our Lord 1854 for the seat of war in the East. On the seventh day's sail, we sighted that stronghold, Gibraltar, where we had some splendid views of the Spanish coasts and other shores on the way to Malta, which noted place we reached on the eleventh day after leaving the shores of England.

HMS Megaera

We cast anchor for a few hours whilst we watered and coaled[1]. The harbour and town was well fortified and offered a safe anchorage for vessels of the largest size which should happen to put in there. As regards the town, it appeared, as far as I was able to judge from board of

---

[1] The ship in question was the HMS Megaera, a screw steamer, hence the need for coal.

ship, to be clean and neatly laid out according to the custom and manners of the people.

After getting sufficient supplies of water, fuel, provisions and other articles necessary for the troops on board, we got under way for the shores of Turkey. Nothing of importance occurred during our voyage up from Malta to Gallipoli, which place we reached in safety and without any incidents on the 16th of May 1854. We cast anchor in the harbour of Gallipoli close to a Turkish vessel of war, where I witnessed a scene that took place on the vessel. It was a scene that not only astonished me, but everyone that beheld it.

It being at this time near sunset, and as we were in a strange country, our decks were crowded with men, and each man was eager to see and hear what was going on around him - the scene that took place that I am about to describe. The sun at this time had nearly disappeared and the shade of night had begun to throw her sable mantle over the face of nature, when suddenly we were startled by a deafening cheer from "Johnny Bono"[2], as they were termed by the allies (our Turkish Comrades). We were surprised to see them, one and all, prostrating themselves on the vessel's deck with their hands clenched about their heads. After remaining in that position for some time they rose on their knees and, as it appeared to us, to go through a form of prayer, bowing themselves frequently to the deck of the vessel. After the sun had finally disappeared, they sprang to their feet and cheered again most lustily. We were a long time before we could make out what they

---

[2] 'Johnny Bono' or 'Bono Johnny' appears to have been a nickname the Turks (and Greeks) used to refer to themselves.

were doing, but we afterwards learned that it was their custom to pay homage to the setting sun.

We disembarked the following morning, this being the 17th day of May in the same year, and marched on through the town of Gallipoli, if a town it can be called, for it was nothing but a wretched collection of huts and cabins roughly thrown together and of the worst material, some built with clay, others with wood and the remainder with a composition of clay, stone, mud and anything else they could lay their hands on to secure a temporary shelter from the rain and heavy dews to which the country is subjected. As regards the streets and passages which led through the town of Gallipoli, they were in a most filthy and dirty condition. The streets were strewed with all kinds of rubbish.

Watercolour of the Gallipoli camp by William Markham (1854)

The town of Gallipoli was inhabited chiefly by Greeks and Bulgarians with a few Americans and Turks, who traded in different branches: some in the public sale of liquor, others dealt in groceries, others in butter, eggs, milk, sweetmeats and different other articles, and they appeared to be driving a good trade at the time the British army were marching through their country on their way to the Crimea.

About noon on the 17th of May, we left Gallipoli and proceeded on our way towards the ground we were to encamp upon. There was a portion of the French army encamped about two miles from the town of Gallipoli and, when our column came up to their camp, they turned out of their tents and gave us a hearty cheer, and numbers of the men came over to our ranks and shook hands with us, and procured lights for our pipes, and gave us what we were much in need of - good water, which much refreshed us - and they did it with seeming kindness and good nature, considering that this was the first time that England and France met together as brothers in arms.

After a severe and fatiguing march through mud and mire, and over uneven roads, we came to the ground we were to encamp upon. We there pitched off our heavy knapsacks on the ground, piled our arms, took off our accoutrements and began to prepare the ground for pitching our tents. That being done and our sentries placed on their posts for the safety of all our troops, we sat down to get a little refreshment after the fatigue of the day. Nor was it long 'ere the floors of our tents were covered with bread, butter, eggs and plenty of good wine, both red and white (for fourpence per quart) and as this was the first time of our being on the Turkish soil, we were determined to make ourselves as comfortable as circumstances would permit and, there being an abundance of good wine at hand, we did not fail to do so. After drinking to the health of our wives and sweethearts and our friends at home, and offering up a prayer to the Throne of Mercy for success against our foes, we threw ourselves down upon our beds of clay and slept like warriors, until aroused by the drums beating to arms at daylight the following morning.

We remained there for a short time and, during the time we were there, the sun was very hot and unhealthy. We then received order to proceed to Bulair[3] to relieve the 4th, 28th and 44th Regiments, who were employed there in constructing batteries and throwing up earthworks as a protection against the enemy if needed, which operation we commenced after arriving there.

Lord Raglan

Our chief employment during our stay there was in erecting wooden barracks to serve us as winter quarters if required, but we were not destined to remain there long, as we were allotted for more active service and, after a short stay in Bulair, we received orders to join the Grand Army under the command of Lord Raglan, then stationed in Varna.

---

[3] Modern day Bolayır. The actual spelling in the journal is 'Bullahar'.

2. VARNA: JUNE - SEPTEMBER 1854

On the 22nd June in the same year, we marched from Bulair to Gallipoli and embarked on board HMS Golden Fleece[4] and proceeded on our way to Varna.

HMS Golden Fleece

On the way to the above named, we passed the celebrated place, Constantinople. It was a beautiful morning in June when we first came in sight of it. It really was a beautiful sight to us who saw it for the first time. There was the grand palace of the Sultans[5] and adjoining it was the seraglio harem where he keeps his 369 wives, with mosques, cathedrals and other places of worship of all shapes and sizes. And these, viewed from the river as we

---

[4] The ship's log states: "26th June 1854. Sailed from Verna for Constantinople, after landing the 38th Foot from Scutari."

[5] The sultan at this time was Abdülmecid I.

sailed gently along, afforded one of the most pleasing sights that any eye could behold.

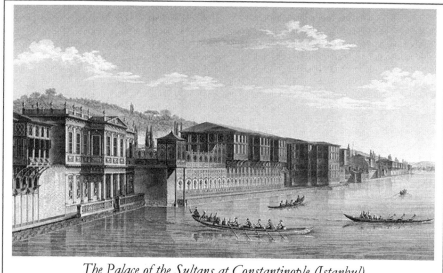

The Palace of the Sultans at Constantinople (Istanbul)

We stayed in the harbour about one hour to leave a few men at Scutari[6] who were sick and, during the short stay, the vessel was surrounded by the inhabitants with bomboats filled with all kinds of fruits, sweetmeats and other articles both pleasing to the eye and suitable to the palate. There was the rich grape, beautiful peaches, apricots, oranges, lemons, apples, nuts, figs, in fact everything that could tempt the beholder to purchase.

After delivering our sick men into the hands of the medical officer stationed there, we then proceeded on our way to Varna and, as we passed through the Bosphorus, the scene was lovely in the extreme around us and we were close to land all the way up, and we enjoyed it very much.

---

[6] Modern Üsküdar - the military hospital made famous by Florence Nightingale.

Guardsmen camping at Scutari before proceeding to Varna

We arrived in Varna on the 26th of June in the evening and disembarked about 9 o'clock the following morning. There we were met by a great number of our comrade soldiers, who welcomed us cheerfully, knowing we had come to take an active part in the trials that awaited us in the East.

We encamped near the Shumla road, about three miles from the town of Varna. At this place, the Army was tolled off into five Divisions, each numbering about five thousand men, not including Cavalry, Artillery or Royal Engineers, which numbered about three thousand more men. We had not been in Varna more than a month when we were reviewed by the Allied Commanders on the plains of Bulgaria, who expressed themselves highly satisfied with our soldier-like appearance and the perfect state of discipline, and they could say that without flattery, for a finer body of men never left the Shores of old England than was assembled on those plains that day: men who were willing and able to meet any equal force in the world.

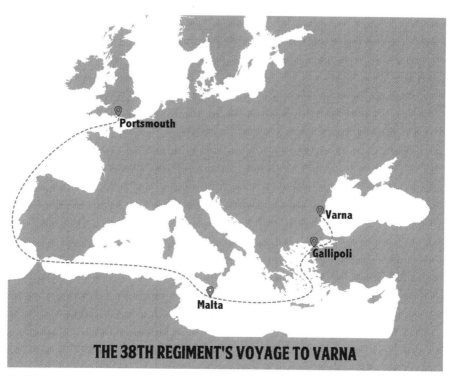

THE 38TH REGIMENT'S VOYAGE TO VARNA

During our stay at Varna, we were employed daily in making roads for the conveyance of our commissariat stores and field equipage from the harbour to the camp, as the Turks never thought of doing anything of the kind themselves. Nor would they assist us unless compelled to do so, which means we often had to resort to as they were most lazy and dirtiest set of people (you may call them savages) in the world, and not worth fighting for. However we managed to change the appearance of them altogether before we left.

At this time the month of June was passed and July came in. It was most intensely hot. The sun was pouring its most powerful heat upon us the whole day long, whilst we were at work, from daylight in the morning until dark at night, in removing our stores and field equipage such as shot, shell, powder, grape, rockets and everything necessary for our campaign.

About the 10th day of this month, the camp was completely darkened with a swarm of locusts. It was about 8 o'clock in the evening that the approach of them was first noticed by a buzzing that much resembled a gale of wind. So great was the number that they destroyed the vines for miles around as they passed through the country. They did not fly more than fourteen or fifteen feet from the ground, and the inhabitants told us that their coming was a sure sign of sickness prevailing amongst us. To our regret we found their statement to be correct for, in the course of a week after we lost sight of them, there was a dreadful disease of that fatal cholera raging through our camps which caused great havoc through our ranks. Really you would think all the men were paralysed. Hundreds of our best men were taken off by it in less than a week from the time it made its first appearance amongst us.

At that time there used generally to sleep in each tent from ten to twelve men. Considering the small space each man occupied, which was only 21 inches in breadth, together with the intense heat of the weather, the tents at night, with the allotted number inside, were almost insufferable. I have seen three or four comrade soldiers, who lay down at night to rest from the heavy fatigues they had gone through during the day, as well in health as they were the day they left the land of their birth, rehearsing to each other the different incidents they had witnessed through the day. A good, merry song would accompany it until they would all fall fast asleep, when everything for a time was forgotten. And then, perhaps at the dead of the night, they would be called upon to call the doctor to the tent or assist in taking the man to the hospital, for once it caught hold of a man it was great misery. Not one alone but perhaps two or three at the same time, their limbs stiffening in death and their features soon changed with the agonising pain that racked their frames. Yet it was scarcely worthwhile taking them to hospital for, when this dreadful disease once got hold of the frame, the grave was his doom. There was no alternative. No cure. No release from the dreadful pains that were racking his frame, until death stepped in and put an end to his sufferings.

A soldier in front of his 12-man tent

Such dreadful scenes of this description have I witnessed that would almost freeze the blood in one's veins, and those poor fellows, who were thousands of miles from their country and friends, lying on a bed of clay and death, where no tender mother or kind father were there to administer to his wants or to soothe him in his suffering. What a contrast between the deathbed of a soldier in the far-off clime, and the one at home. The one at home is surrounded by kind friends and relations. Perhaps father, mother, brothers and sisters all are administering to him as much as possible all his wants, soothing and comforting him in his last departing moments, while the poor Crimean experienced none of these attendants. No, not one. God grant that we may never witness such scenes as I did during my stay in Turkey.

We had now got into the month of August when another calamity, though of another description, caused us to stay longer in Turkey than we should otherwise have done. What occasioned this was an alarming fire that broke out in our stores situated in the town of Varna.

On the 10th of August in the same year and about 8 o'clock in the evening, the allied camps were suddenly alarmed by the cry of "Fire!" The troops were instantly ordered to proceed at once to the scene of conflagration, which at this time could be seen for miles around the place. The first place the fire broke out was at our commissariat stores, but how it originated is not known. The stores were filled with provisions of all kinds, such as biscuit, beef, pork, rum, sugar, tea, coffee and other articles for the use of the troops in abundance. The adjoining building to this was our main magazine, filled with powder, live shells, rockets, shot and other combustibles for siege operations, and had that building caught fire it would have blown all the town and what it contained to atoms, but fortunately it escaped.

With prompt assistance being rendered by the allied powers, everything was soon placed out of the way of the flames and in safety. And when we had done so, we all began to solace ourselves with a cup of good brandy or wine as it was running down the street in hogsheads, which the troops, both English and French, partook of freely. The fire was not properly extinguished for nearly a week, during which time we were employed in getting our stores on board a ship, preparatory to our leaving Varna, that British Grave Yard; such it had proved to be for hundreds of brave Englishmen.

A group of Tatars employed by the Allied army

At this time, we have everything in readiness to leave this

fatal place of disease and death. But before quitting it, I will endeavour to give a faint idea of the customs and manners of the inhabitants. I will first begin with Johnny Bono himself. They are dirty, lazy, slothful and wretched savages.

The man's dress is a follows: his head is covered with a kind of rough furze cap, such as I never saw in England or Ireland, and as regards the make or shape of it, and the way it is worn exceeds anything I ever saw. There is then several yards of cotton cloth wound round closely to the head, what is called in that country a turban. Next, there is no hair on their heads, only a small tuft just on the crown, something like a cats tail. They are under the opinion that they will be drawn up to heaven by that when they die. Next comes the coat or jacket. It's of a very rough kind of sacking, variegated all over with different coloured lace or braid, something like a merry man's in a pantomime on the stage of some theatre, with the sleeves hanging useless by their shoulders. Next what they term Cacklimonies.[7] They are made something after the manner of an English woman's petticoat, tied around the waist with a strong cord and sewn at the bottom, leaving a small hole at the two corners to put their two feet and legs through. It reaches to their knees. Next the feet. They cut a piece of horse or buffalo hide to the shape of the foot, cut small holes all around it and, with a thong of the same material, it is drawn tight to the ankle. Their whole breast and legs are exposed to the intense heat of the unhealthy climate.

---

[7] Richard seems to be referring here to the Shalvar, the traditional baggy trousers of the Tatars. Where he got the word 'Cacklimonies' from is a mystery to me.

Now for that fair sex, the women. They are clothed generally in a loose, white garment that covers them from head to foot. The head is covered with a large white handkerchief which conceals all the face, except those two bright eyes, which always attract the attention of anyone who might see them passing. Their feet are covered with a pair of red morocco slippers. As regards their good looks, I cannot say much, as I had not the opportunity of seeing many of them. But it happened one morning during my tour of duty on the main guard of Varna, I was surprised to see a beautiful young woman pass close to my post. She was at that time about seventeen years of age. She was beautifully dressed after the manner I have just described to you. I had not the time to take much notice of her, for she passed my post so quick, but I judged by the appearance of her that she possessed her own share of what our lasses at home are so proud of (I mean beauty). So much for the male and female of Turkey.

A few words now on their mode of agriculture. I happened one evening to be taking a walk through some of the vineyards not far from our camp, when my attention was called to an old woman who, with two buffaloes, seemed to be driving something in the shape of a plough. For you must know that the women in the country are like the old Indians, doing all the work that their husbands should perform as in ancient times. My curiosity tempted me to draw a little nearer to the old lady in order to ascertain what she was doing and, in going up to her, I found she was ploughing. But it was the shape and make of the plough that took my attention. First there was a kind of yoke fastening round the neck of the animals, something in the shape of a short stepladder, and a long pole connecting that to the plough. The next thing I observed was that there was no iron used in any part of it, not even the share. In fact, I don't think there was any. It only had one handle and the old lady seemed as if she was taking it very easy, not the least concerned about anything. They used no reins, the animals moved and stopped by words of mouth.

Another time, I was taking my evening walk and I saw a large ring of hurdles formed something like a circus, with about forty or fifty animals, such as horses, bullocks, buffaloes, dromedaries, camels, asses, in fact anything with four legs inside the ring that I just mentioned. In the ring there was corn thrown on the ground and these animals galloped round as fast as they were able to go and there was a driver in with them with a whip, keeping them up to speed. When they were satisfied that the corn was all out of the ear, it was then put on a cart and removed to their dwelling. The straw is all like chaff and no good for the many things that the British find it useful. I will not delay any longer on these uncultivated wretches; they are not worth it.

3. ARRIVAL IN THE CRIMEA: SEPTEMBER 1854

The Landing at Calamita Bay by William Simpson (1854)

On the 3rd of September, the whole of the British troops were on board the different ships that were to convey them to the Crimean shores from those of Turkey. At the appointed hour for sailing, the whole of the allied fleet, numbering about three hundred vessels of war, left Balchic Bay, a place appointed to meet by Divisions: the Light Division leading, followed by the 1st, 2nd, 3rd[8] and 4th Divisions in succession. And a noble sight it was to see such a number of vessels on the bosom of the deeps at one time, and all in their proper places, freighted with about eight thousand troops besides the marines and the ships' crews. Indeed, I have heard some of the oldest marines say that such a fleet and army never was on the waters under

---

[8] The 38th Regiment was in the 3rd Division.

(you may say) the one commander before. While on the water, there was nothing of importance that occurred during our passage from Varna to the Crimea shores, which lasted 14 days[9].

The Landing Area of Calamita Bay

On the evening of the 13th September, we came in sight of those shores. We then prepared for landing. On the following morning about 12 o'clock, we commenced the disembarkation. Every vessel landed its own regiment by means of boats that were brought for the purpose. At the above named hour, the landing commenced and we expected to meet with a warm reception from our yet unknown enemy, but they kept at a respectful distance from us and allowed us to step on their shores without opposition. After landing we marched a short distance from the sea beach and each division took up its position for the night, and after throwing out pickets, posting

[9] Though the journey from Varna to Calamita Bay is only three hundred miles, it apparently took two weeks due to Lord Raglan's indecision over where to land.

guards and making everything as secure as military experience could suggest, we piled arms, put on our watch coats and prepared to make ourselves as comfortable as circumstances would admit. We threw ourselves down on the cold ground and, after being cooped up on board ship, you may depend we were not long before being asleep.

Arms piled outside the tents

But before I resigned myself to sleep, my thoughts wandered towards home, where all I loved so dear dwelt comfortable, sleeping in their beds surrounded by the family circle, except me. And my head tells me that the prayer, for protection through all the difficulties and dangers that awaited me through the campaign, was offered up to the Throne of Mercy for the absent one. At length, like my commanders who were lying around me, I fell into a deep slumber.

How long I slept I do not know, but this I do know, that I was awoke by the rain descending in torrents upon our shelterless heads. Every man was up on his feet directly, thinking to find some shelter that would protect us from the drenching rain that was falling heavily upon us. But alas there was none to be found, for we were encamped upon a barren heath of vast extent and not a tree, shrub or bush within miles of our bivouac. So, to protect ourselves as much as possible, we threw three of our blankets on the top of our piles of arms, and each three men crept under these piles of arms, but this did not offer us much protection from the pitiless storm that was raging around us.

At this time, daylight had made its appearance and the rain somewhat abated. We then, to make our situation a little more comfortable, began to look around us to see if anything in the shape of fuel could be found in this dreary spot that would enable us to make a fire. But nothing of the kind was to be seen, for there was scarcely a blade of grass to be seen around our whole bivouac. So we had no alternative but to send out parties in search of something of the sort, which was accordingly done. But all was in vain, for there was none within miles of us. But still something must be done, for we began to feel the cravings of hunger at this time stealing upon us, and we knew that we must either get wood or go without our breakfast, which was not to be thought of. So we changed our line of march and steered for the place where we landed to see if we could pick up anything that might have washed ashore with the waves, that would serve us for our present difficulties. But we saw nothing there that we dared meddle with. But in going about a mile further along the beach, we found five or six fisherman's boats, belonging to the Russians. But what to do in our present situation we did not know. (They were almost as sour to us, as the grapes were to the fox). There was plenty of wood in front of us, but it was the property of another, although that other was our enemy.

But still we did not know how far we might be justified in destroying those boats. Yet we must either do that or go without our breakfast, which was not to be thought of.

So to work we went and, with the aid of some large stones that were fortunately at hand, the boats were soon demolished and every man in the party loaded with as much as he could stand under, wending his way to the bivouac, which we had no sooner reached than we began to consider, after getting the wood, how we were to set fire to it. But as necessity is the mother of invention, a plan was soon adopted to ignite it, which was done in this manner.

One brave fellow cried, "Here. Here's my shirt. A good breakfast is better than a bad shirt any day. Take this and light the fire with it." No sooner said than done. In about one moment it was all in shreds, so that it would be a difficult task to put it together again. Now with this and the aid of a percussion cap, taken from our pouches and half-filled with powder, we then placed it on the point of one of our ramrods with a piece of rag round it, and a smart tap of the bayonet caused the cap to explode and the rag to ignite. That being placed under the dry wood, two or three of us, going down on our knees, began puffing away like a pig in a fit, until we had succeeded in blowing it into a flame so that, in a short time, we had the pleasure of seeing a cheerful, blazing fire in front of us. And I assure you, my reader, it was not before it was wanted, for we were all wet through from the rain that fell in torrents the night previous.

It was now about 5 o'clock in the morning and the troops, both officers and men, were gathered around a cheerful fire. The gay laugh and merry jest told plainly that the unpleasant situation of the night was nearly forgotten after enjoying the comfort of the fire for some time and, by this time, our clothes being very nearly all dry.

Soldiers enjoying coffee in the Crimea

The sun began to make its appearance, which aided us greatly in drying our watch coats and blankets. It was then thought advisable to begin to look after something in the shape of a breakfast. Parties were sent out in search of water, but found none except what they gathered from the horse tracks and wheel marks that our cavalry and artillery had made the day previous and which were luckily filled by the rain of the night before; although it caused us all to wear wet clothes almost the whole day before we could get them dry, it was by the means of it that we were enabled to procure a breakfast. The water was both muddy and dirty but, as there was no better to be found, we had to make the best of it. So the camp kettles were brought into play and, in a short time, the whole of us were as pleased as a child with a penny rattle, because the breakfast was ready.

I only wish some of my friends at home could have partaken with me a portion of the delicious breakfast that was laid on the table (ground) before us. It consisted of wet biscuits soaked from the rain the night previous and coffee well thickened with the sand that was mixed with the water gathered from the rucks and tracks in the road. You would actually think by its colour that it was nicely flavoured with milk yet, as bad as it was, we thought it as good a breakfast as need be. There was no difference between the officers and the men. Here Jack was as good as his master, that being the first meal that the British troops partook of on the Crimean shores.

After we finished our breakfast, we spread out our blankets and watch coats to dry by the fire that there was no trouble in fetching or looking for wood to keep burning: the Sun. We had several pieces of dirty linen in our knapsacks at this time and began to consider how we were to clean them without the soap or water that was generally used, for we had none or any means of procuring any. That was no easy task, to wash without either soap or water, but as the proverb says, "Time and perseverance will overcome all obstacles." Either way, we had nothing but perseverance to depend upon at the time, so we turned our knapsacks over and tied its contents in a towel and trudged on towards the sea beach. On arriving there, we stripped ourselves naked and plunged into the surging waves, taking our clothes with us. Then, taking one piece out of the bundle and placing the bundle under our feet to prevent the waves from washing it away, we began to beat our shirts and drawers, whichever it was, well in the sand with a large stone, until we had got them pretty clean of the dirt from our voyage. We afterwards rinsed them in the waves as they rolled past us, to and fro. Then we spread them on the beach to dry, which did not take long as the sun cast a great heat at this time, September 15th 1854.

Our troops, both Cavalry and Infantry, were all landed and encamped on the bank of Lake Touzla[10], where we remained for three days. During our stay there, a portion of our Light Division captured a large quantity of flour from the Russians on their way to Alma.

Captain Vam of the 38th Regiment

---

[10] I have failed to identify this lake, but it is mentioned in several other books (e.g. The Durham Light Infantry by W L Vane, and Historical Record of the Forty-Fourth by Thomas Carter), so I've left it unchanged. The lake nearest to where the troops landed was referred to as Kamishlu, but Richard may be referring to one of the smaller salt lakes nearby.

I must tell you, my reader, what the Catholics did for the Protestants one Sunday during divine service. The Catholics were usually at home from prayers before the Protestants' Service began. On this day, the different regiments of the division were formed up in square, listening (or should have been) to what was being said by the clergyman, when all at once there came into the camp a fine drove of sheep, about 150 in number. The sight of them made our mouths water, as fresh meat was rather scarce amongst us at this time, it being more than a month since we tasted any and perhaps a long time before we should have the opportunity again. But we (Protestants) could not move from where we were. Not so the Catholics.

A soldier considering a Crimean sheep

As soon as they saw them, they made a general rush at the whole flock and, in a short time, not one of the number was to be seen. You would see one fellow with a sheep, another with a goat, staggering under its weight towards the camp where its bleating was soon put a stop to, by drawing a knife across its neck, the body distributed through the Company and, in a very short time, there could be seen chops cooking in all directions and every man had the opportunity of getting as much mutton that day as he required.

On the evening of the 18th of September, we received orders to march at daybreak the following morning and, before daylight appeared, every man was roused from his slumber by the beating of drums to arms, that being then about three o'clock a.m.

Each division was formed up on their own ground when the order was given to advance in column, which was accordingly done. The French were on the right, next to the sea, the British on the left. As for the Turks, I did not see them. Our march was covered by a brigade of Rifles, thrown out in skirmishing order.

The troops left Lake Touzla that morning without either provisions or water, yet we left with light hearts and excellent spirits. We marched a considerable distance before the sun, which at that time of the year is very powerful, began to make us rather warm. About 12 o'clock in the day, the sun was pouring its burning rays upon us. It was then that we began to feel the want of water, of the cooling beverage, but up to that hour there was none to be had. The men, some of them being very young and this being the first time a great many of them had ever experienced such severity and scarcity, began to fall to the rear of the columns in hundreds, being unable to keep up for the want of refreshment. Still the older hands pushed on without a murmur until, at length, some of those were obliged to give up for the want of the same beverage, and exhaustion compelled them to lay down at last, gasping for breath. The Generals, seeing that so many of the men were falling out of the ranks, were afraid that none of them would be able to proceed much further unless water could be procured. A halt was therefore called and aids sent out in different directions to see if any was to be found. After searching for some time, they returned with the pleasing intelligence that what we dreadfully wanted was to be had about a mile from where we were then. The order was given to fall in and proceed towards the place where it could be obtained.

We had then been marching about nine hours in the burning sun without a drop to wet our lips or cool our tongues, in fact without tasting bib or sup of any kind and over rough and uneven ground with a heavy knapsack, our accoutrements, along with 60 rounds of ammunition. Indeed, our tongues were swollen in our mouths, our lips parched and scarcely able to mutter a word.

Artillery wagons used by the Allied Troops

At length, the word was given to halt and unpack, and never was an order obeyed with more alacrity than was that welcome word: "Fall out". Such a charge was never seen as was made, by the whole army, to reach that muddy and dirty stream of water; it was both, for our Cavalry, Artillery, land transport, ararbas[11], bullocks and bullock trucks had passed through it before we could reach it ourselves. But it was sweeter to our parched throats at that time than the best of brandy. I think if some of our fellow countrymen had witnessed the scene, they would have pitied any soldier in that unhealthy climate. We were up to our boot tops in water, some with canteens, lamps, kettles, tin cups or water bottles and others with their hands, selecting the cleanest drops they could find in that muddy stream. It was a difficult task for us to slake our burning thirst. I myself thought I should never have had enough, so refreshing was it to our exhausted frames. But, like everything else, it must have an end. So it was with us, but not before we were well cautioned by our officers of the risk we ran of getting the cramps in our bowels. We halted about an hour at the stream, dirty as it was, that had given us so much satisfaction and enabled us to quench our thirst. Not only that, but we had plenty of time to fill our pipes and take a comfortable smoke, stretching at full length on the grass. Nor did we neglect in filling our water bottles for fear we should get no more that night, for we did not know how far we had to march that day.

We had not advanced more than a mile when, all of a sudden, we were startled by a booming of cannon on our

---

[11] A heavy wagon or cart used by the Turks

right, which made every man slip into his place in a moment, thinking we were about to have a brush with the enemy. But we were mistaken. The French though were not, as they had to shell a frontier of the Russians out of a small fort which lay direct in their line of march. It did not last long nor were there any lives lost on our side, but there were three or four of the cavalry wounded, this being the first brush between our Cavalry and the Cossacks.

Shortly after this, a halt was called on the ground where we were to bivouac for the night. After we had halted, strong pickets were thrown out, guards posted and every necessary precaution taken to prevent surprises, as the enemy lay only a short distance from us. It was now near sunset and, our commissariat having come up with the column, the rations were served out to the troops as soon as possible, for we had been then about 40 hours without anything to eat and marching all the day from about 4 o'clock that morning until sunset the same evening, through the heat of the day which would very near melt an old soldier's metal buttons.

Fortunately for us, the ground we encamped upon was thickly strewn with heaps of dry weeds, briers, thistles, grass and stubble so that, in a short time, hundreds of fires could be seen blazing around our bivouacs. I will leave the reader to judge the number of fires when every 3 or 4 men had one to themselves, out of 25,000 British and about 30,000 French troops. The camp kettles were brought into play and we soon had sufficient food cooked to satisfy our hunger. And what did us as much, or more, good was a good glass of Commissariat rum issued to every man in the army.

After partaking of that meal of salt pork and biscuit, we began to prepare our beds for the night by collecting some of the same material that the fires were made with and shaking it nicely on the ground, with the Watch Coats and blankets thrown over us; this made us an excellent bed. After the fatigue of the day's march, we slept that night with our arms by our side ready for use in a moment. Nor was it long before the greater part of our wearied soldiers were fast asleep, their toils and fatigue of the day forgotten in a deep and well-earned repose. Not so with myself for, as I lay on the ground my head pillowed by my knapsack, I thought how many of the brave fellows, who lay around me and who were in possession of life and good health, had, I have no doubt, lifted their vows in prayer to the Almighty for protection through the deadly struggle, which every man knew was to take place the following day at the Alma, distant about five miles from where we then were. Yes, before the expiration of another day, thousands of the brave fellows and hearts that were then beating with life and hope would fall to rise no more, their bodies left to moulder in the earth, red with their blood shed in defence of their country.

4. BATTLE OF ALMA: 20 SEPTEMBER 1854

We lay undisturbed by the side of our arms until the shrill notes of the bugle called us to be ready for the march. It was about five o'clock a.m. on the 20th day of September, a day that never will be forgotten by any man who escaped from the dreadful scenes that were enacted on the bloody heights of Alma.

The British army, both officers and men, wore quite a different appearance that morning to what they did the night before, for then they were weary and fatigued after a hard day's march and want of refreshment, but in the morning they rose forth after a good night's rest and were prepared to confront any difficulty, however dangerous, that may offer itself. The officers too seemed well pleased with the men under their several commands.

The Heights of Alma

The order to march was given to the different divisions about seven o'clock in the morning, and every man that was on the ground knew that the honour of England was in their hands and what England expected from her sons there assembled. They marched boldly forward with a determination to curb the insolence of the grasping foe or perish in the attempt.

It was about eleven o'clock in the day when we first sighted the heights of Alma and the immense force of Russians that crowned them. It took us a considerable time to get into a position favourable for an attack. The enemy, in the meantime, kept a watchful eye upon all our movements and seemed to be waiting quite easily for our approach. Nor did we delay, for one moment longer than was necessary, to form up in order of battle. This being done, the 2nd Battalion of the Rifle Brigade was ordered to advance in skirmishing order to cover the front of our army.

The enemy no sooner saw this than they set fire to the village that lay at the foot of the heights, on this side of the river, so as to impede the advance of our Rifles. The village was deserted by its inhabitants and their dwellings were filled with straw to which the enemy set fire. The Rifles were not more than a quarter of a mile from the village when clouds of smoke and fire from the houses burst upon their view and completely hid them for a time from the anxious gaze of their comrades. Yet, in spite of all and every obstacle that was thrown in their way, did these brave fellows push their way through the burning village, supported by the Light Division, who formed lines in front of the enemy on the heights above them and poured into their ranks a destructive fire of musketry. The Artillery of the enemy were throwing in grape and round shot upon our advancing columns, but could not stay their progress.

By this time, our advance of Rifles had succeeded in driving the Russian sharpshooters across the river at the foot of the heights and in getting into their trenches, which they had thrown up for their protection, with considerable loss to the enemy. The battle lasted at this time about an hour. The light division had been relieved by the 1st at this time, and the men were falling on both sides very fast. Our artillery had got within range and made fearful havoc in the dense masses of the enemy. So correct was their range and so close were they to the enemy that they literally made lanes through their columns.

The battle at this time became general. The 1st and 2nd Divisions had been engaged and were about to be relieved by the 3rd. When they were in line and advancing, a wavering could be seen in the enemy columns and they were seen to recoil from the deadly aim of our Minié rifle. It was then that the general order was given for the whole of the British troops to advance and drive the foe from a position that their commanders had told them no power in the world could do. And never shall I forget the sight that that battlefield presented, a sight that the whole or nearly the whole of the British army had. For the first time there lay thousands of the brave fellows, who a short time before could boast of life, health and strength, dead on the gory plains of bloody Alma.

It would have surprised anyone could they have seen how cooly our brave allies, the French, ascended those heights in front of a superior force to their own. And under a galling fire from the enemy's batteries that were playing upon them, they still kept on their way, fighting for every foot of ground they passed over, while dozens of their men fell at every discharge from the enemy's guns, which greatly thinned their ranks. Still on they went and, after a dreadful struggle, succeeded in turning their enemies left and getting into their batteries, while the British took the centre and right.

Prince Alexander Menchikov, the Russian Commander-in-Chief

There was great credit due to the Fleet, who assisted greatly in shelling the enemy off the Heights. The French had no sooner got possession of the enemy's works on the left, than they turned the guns upon the Russians, who were already flying from the field, throwing down their arms and knapsacks as they went along the rear to enable them to get out of the reach of shot, shell and musketry, which was making fearful havoc in the retreating columns. The infantry, both French and English, pursued them from the foot to the top of the hill, or heights, driving them at the point of the bayonet from the position they had fought so hard to retain.

So sure were the Russian commanders that they could hold those Heights and maintain the position against all the force that could be brought to bear upon them, that Prince Menshikov duly invited a large party of his friends to see his troops drive the "English heretics", as he termed them, into the sea. But they did not stay to see that part of the fun and, when our shot and shell began to find their way towards them, they, like the sensible people as they were, made the best of their way towards a place of safety and left their friend, the Prince, and his swarms of men endeavouring to keep the British Lion from the Russian Eagle. But all in vain. He could not stop the advance nor check the daring spirits that animated the breast of the British soldier. Onwards they went, with the standard of England floating proudly in the ranks, borne by the men who had that day so nobly done their duty. In spite of opposition and overwhelming numbers, we succeeded in driving the enemy from the position they so proudly boasted in the morning that no force could do, thousands of his men laying dead or dying around him, several of his generals and officers were killed and taken prisoner, himself flying over the plain of Alma's heights, his army routed and pursued by a victorious foe. And this was done in 3 hours or thereabouts.

Now, where the double-headed Eagle of Russia floated so proudly in the early part of the day, the British flag, the symbol of victory, waved triumphantly.

So ended the Battle of Alma, fought on the 20th September 1854.

Heights of Alma the Day After Battle by Joseph Benwell (1854)

5. MARCH TO SEVASTOPOL: 21 - 27 SEPTEMBER 1854

That night we encamped on the heights overlooking the battle plains and, as it was late when we got into position for the night, we had no opportunity of visiting the field of fight. But no rest could we get, as it was dreadful to hear the cries of the poor fellows, who lay desperately wounded beneath us.

At daylight the following morning, strong parties were sent out to render assistance to the wounded and to inter the dead, a melancholy task for the survivors of the previous day's slaughter. There lay our comrades in heaps, intermingled with those of the French and the Russians. It was a sickening sight and it took us two days before the dead were interred and the wounded placed in a position as to be attended to by the medical officers, who were left there for that purpose.

This being done and all the arms that were fit for service destroyed, we were ordered to hold ourselves in readiness to march on the morning of the 23rd of the same month, which we did according to orders, leaving the heights of Alma to encounter fresh difficulties and dangers that we knew lay before us.

We proceeded and, on our way over mountainous country, kept a sharp lookout to guard against surprise. Nothing of importance occurred during the day and at night we halted on the Belbek.[12]

---

[12] The river Bel'bek is roughly 11 miles south of the river Alma

38

It was a very nice place as there was plenty of fruit of all kinds and a good supply of vegetables, which were most wel-come to us, and we were able to have an excellent meal after halting. We afterwards took a stroll in the dif-ferent orchards and vineyards that lay around us and partook of some of the finest fruits as

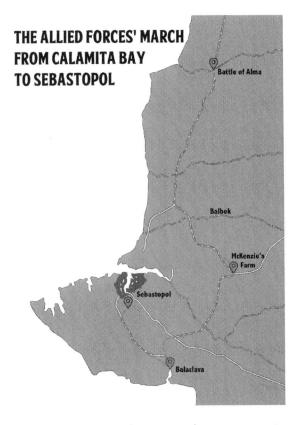

THE ALLIED FORCES' MARCH FROM CALAMITA BAY TO SEBASTOPOL

Battle of Alma

Balbek

McKenzie's Farm

Sebastopol

Balaclava

ever was eaten, such as grapes, peaches, apples, pears; in fact it was too numerous to mention.

Next morning at sunrise, we were again roused to proceed on our way and, after a heavy day's march over hill, dale, valley and mountain, without incident, we again halted for the night, in the midst of a thick bush, extending as far as we could see. We were situated on the top of a hill, several hundred feet above the level of the sea. At daylight the morning notes of the bugle roused us from our usual slumbers, to prepare again for the march. After collecting some dry wood from the bottom of the bushes, as there was plenty there, we made fires and cooked some coffee, but had no biscuit to eat with it. We had only half an hour, so we had to do it in quick time. We were ordered to stand to our arms, fall in and prepare for the road.

So we were on our way through the bush, a thick forest with no regular order of march, for the place we were marching through would not admit it as there was no path to guide our steps and the only way we had of getting on at all was by a bugler being stationed at the head of the respective regiment and sounding from time to time their regimental call, which was understood by the men and enabled them to keep together. But still that did not prevent a great many of our men from falling out to the rear. So difficult was the task to get along, there was a great many men left in the bush and were never heard of any more. I suppose they fell into the hands of the enemy.

After several hours' march, we came upon one of the enemy's outposts, called McKenzie's Farm, but on the approach of our Cavalry, who were in front, and after exchanging a few shots with them, they abandoned the fort and retired into the bush, followed by a company of Rifles, who succeeded in capturing a few. And dispersing the others, I suppose, as we heard nothing of them during the night.

We halted there and, on making a tour round the place, a large quantity of flour was discovered in a large store room but, as we could not make use of it, it was all destroyed. When we halted, it was thought by all classes that we should have stayed there for the night and we began to prepare for it accordingly by lighting fires to enable us to get some refreshment, for we stood very much in need of it, for we had tasted nothing since four o'clock in the morning up to the present hour. Nor did we get anything then for, just as we were in the act of cooking our meal, the bugle sounded for us to fall in, which we did and without noise, not knowing what it was for. But we were not kept long in suspense as the order to advance was soon given, which you may be sure was anything but a welcome order to us, as we were faint with hunger. But there was no help for it but to pack up our traps and proceed on our way. It was now that I began to experience some of the pleasures of a campaign.

We marched the whole of that night through some of the wildest passes I ever saw in my life. There was a chain of mountains on each side of us, which offered beautiful cover for an enemy to lay in ambush, and we were given to understand afterwards that they were not more than one or two miles from us during the whole night's march. How it was that we did not come in contact with them during the night, I do not know.

About three o'clock in the morning, we got clear of these close and narrow roads, and came at last on the plains of Biadar and thankful we were that we did so, for the troops were worn out from fatigue and exhaustion, our tongues swollen almost too large for our mouths from the dust of the roads and want of water. It was about 5 o'clock in the morning before we came to a halt. It was on a very large plain about six miles from Balaclava.

When the men were halted, their knapsacks taken off and arms piled, some of the men who were able set about cooking their breakfast, while others, who were unable to do so, threw themselves on the ground to rest their weary limbs after the severe fatigue attending the forced night's march. But, like the night before, just when the men had got fires lighted and had begun to get ready the meal, we received orders to be as quick as possible with our preparations for we had still further to go. Accordingly, every man who was not too much fatigued busied himself in getting his or their meal ready, and anyone seeing them then, and seeing them two hours before, would not have thought they had been the same men. For, at one time, they were completely beat up, hardly able to set one leg before the other but, as soon as there was a prospect of getting what they stood in need of so badly (rest and refreshment), they were quite a different party of men altogether, both officers and men, as their bivouac proved them to be in a very short time after the halt was called.

Meal time for the soldiers

We had not been halted more than an hour when rations were served out, fires lit and the camp kettles were sending forth a delicious smell, which served to bring our weary and fatigued soldiers to their feet, as there was every prospect of a good breakfast being set before them.

The village of Biadar was well stocked with all kinds of vegetables and you may be sure that we did not forget to welcome ourselves to as much as was necessary for our own use. Both officers and men were anxiously looking forward to that word which should announce to us that the meal was ready. Nor had we to wait long before the magic word was uttered, when we all fell to, to satisfy an appetite of 36 hours' duration. And you may depend that we did it ample justice.

Immediately after breakfast, the gill of grog was issued to us. As soon as that was done, the order was given to fall in and continue our march. Certainly there was not a man in the army, from the Commander in Chief downwards, who would have liked very much to stay there for that day at least, but it was not to be our destination. So away we started, all in excellent spirits, although it was but a short stay of rest. The bands struck up with a lively air of 'Over the Hills and Far Away' and we bid adieu to the Plains of Biadar.

After marching about two hours, we came in sight of the castle of Balaclava, then in ruins, as our advanced guard, with the assistance of the fleet, soon brought its defenders to their senses and the walls of their stronghold down about their ears.

We halted that day on the Plains of Balaclava amidst vineyards, orchards and crops of every description, and everything about the place seemed to announce that the inhabitants of that place were comfortably situated. After resting ourselves a short time, some of us thought it advisable to take a view of the town and harbour.

Balaclava Castle viewed from the harbour

The town consisted only of a few scattered huts apparently belonging to fisherman, with a few small farmhouses amongst them. As regards the harbour of Balaclava, it is small, but it has a safe anchorage for vessels of the largest size. The British took possession of it, and it was there that all the stores, both for the Commissariat and our camp equipage, all our guns, shot, shell and everything required for the campaign, was landed and conveyed to the front of Sebastopol. Balaclava is about 7 or 8 miles from the town of Sebastopol, to which we received orders to proceed the following morning. After a good night's rest, we prepared for the road. We partook of breakfast and left the plains of Balaclava for Sebastopol.

6. SEBASTOPOL: 27 SEPTEMBER - 16 OCTOBER 1854

It was on the 27th of September that the British army arrived in front of that formidable place, Sebastopol. We were two or three days moving about before we got finally into position. The Light and 1st Division took up a position on the extreme right of the British lines, the 2nd and 4th Division in the centre and rear, near to Cathcart's Hill (as it was termed from a general being killed and buried there), and the Third Division were placed on the extreme left of the British lines.

Cathcart's Hill

The camp of the 3rd Division was posted on a high hill, in the midst of beautiful orchards, vineyards, splendid plantations and costly-built dwelling houses, belonging to the gentry of that neighbourhood, and those houses announced to us, when we first came in sight of them, that the inmates were doing well. In fact, the gardens and houses denoted wealth and comfort. Yet, a few weeks after the British army sat down before Sebastopol, those beautiful edifices and stately mansions, with these rich vineyards, orchards, flower gardens, plantations and everything else, were torn down and pulled to pieces to supply the troops with fuel to cook their meals, and the owners of those happy homes, once surrounded by their families and friends and in possession of everything that makes life desirable, were driven, perhaps with their wives and little ones, to seek the shelter and protection in another clime that they could not find in their own. Such is war.

From the 27th of September to the 9th of October we were bivouacked in the open air with nothing to cover us but our watch coats and one blanket. The weather at that time was getting very chilly and damp from the heavy dews that fell during the night.

Our chief concentration was on the town and, if one man asked another how long he thought it would be before we would get the Russians out of it, some would say one thing and some another. Perhaps up would come an artilleryman to look at the town.

"Well," he'd say, "I understand we are going to lay siege to it and, if we do, I am sure that all and every one of those houses will fall to the ground in about 24 hours, and then it will belong to the British soon after."

Perhaps before he had done giving his speech, up would come an Infantry solider.

"Well, boys, I understand we are going to storm the town in two or three days and, if we do, we will be in possession of it in about 12 or 24 hours."

It went on very well until it was tried, and everyone could see that the proof of the pudding was in the eating of it.

On the 9th of October, our Brigadier, Sir John Campbell (now no more), called our attention to what we were going to do.

Sir John Campbell sitting outside his tent

He told us that we were going to break ground in front of the enemy so as to enable the Engineers to erect batteries to answer those of the enemy, which had for three or four days previous been playing upon us, throwing their shot and shell into our very camp, but fortunately doing us little or no damage. His orders to us were to proceed as quickly as possible to our destination, guided by a party of Royal Sappers and Miners. When there, we were to work like cats until we had succeeded in throwing up a sufficient cover to protect us from the enemy's fire.

It was about 10 o'clock at night, when a party of men, 1500 strong, belonging to the 3rd Division, left their camp for the purpose above named and the greatest silence prevailed in our ranks. We proceeded in this way until we came within about one mile of the enemy's works. Each man had with him one pick, one shovel and one gabion, or large basket.

Gabions being made in the Crimea - London Illustrated News (1855)

These we were ordered to fill with earth, after which all were placed in line so as to form a cover for ourselves. The night, being dark, prevented us from being seen by the enemy or, I expect, we should have received a salute from them rather disagreeable to us for the first night, but we continued to work unmolested the whole night. We were all at work from about 11 o'clock at night until about four the next morning.

A trench was thrown up four feet deep, six feet wide

and about one and a half miles long. Daylight now began to appear and we left the ground without incident and reached our camp in safety. The enemy, I have no doubt, were surprised in the morning, when they saw what had been done in the night.

That night's work enabled our Engineers to work in safety at their batteries, which they did both night and day, assisted by large working parties from all the camps around in their turns. Our guns were all brought from Balaclava in daylight and left at a convenient place until dark, and then removed to the works at night and mounted in the Batteries.

Ordnance stored at Balaclava

The powder, shot and shell were brought up in the same way, and magazines were made to put it into as it was brought up from the stores. This was done amid showers of shot and shell, accompanied by difficulties and dangers to all those who were engaged in it. Still the work was carried on with rapidity. There could be seen several batteries ready for use or to open fire on the enemy whenever the order to do so should be given. The French were making preparations too for the day the siege should open. The troops in the meantime were working night and day in the trenches, aiding the Engineers in making the works as strong as possible. The enemy, during the erection of our batteries, kept up a constant fire on the parties so employed.

A Russian cannon, captured at Sevastopol
(now in Ely)

On the evening of the 16th of October, the batteries were reported to be ready for use both in our lines and those of the French, so it was determined by the Commander in Chief and his Generals that they should open fire for the first time on that Russian stronghold, Sebastopol.

7. THE SIEGE OF SEBASTOPOL BEGINS: 17 - 22 OCT 1854

On the morning of the 17th, about 3,000 men paraded in front of the respective camps. As a guard for the trenches, we were marched to the works at an early hour and, when there, we were ordered to keep as close to our breastworks as possible and to lay our arms beside us so that there could be no delay in laying our hand upon them if required. The Gunners were busy in preparations for the deathly work that was about to take place. The embrasures were all opened and the formidable works of the enemy, bristling with cannon, could be seen by us if we rose our heads a little above the trenches, but it was rather dangerous for anyone to do so as the enemy saw clearly what we were about and saluted us with a heavy discharge of ordnance from every gun they could bring to bear upon us, knocking some men over as they stood impatiently at their guns, waiting for orders from their officers to return the compliment.

It was about six o'clock in the morning when the General Officer on duty ordered them to load their guns and open fire, which was no sooner said than done. At it they went. Every man's heart beat high when the sound of their own guns reached their ears. But it was not long before death made its appearance among our men in the batteries from the shot and shell that the enemy threw amongst us, as thick as a shower of hail. It was a dreadful sight to witness the deaths that took place that day in the trenches. I have seen more than one or two of our artillerymen going to and from the magazines for changes of powder, who would be struck with a round shot or shell and perhaps his body cut in two or his head, arm or leg taken off and there lay in front of our eyes either dead or dying until taken to the rear by his comrades.

The Enemy's Guns

The fire from our batteries continued with great vigour upon the enemy's works for about four hours, when one of the forts, called the Round Tower, which was made of stone, was completely levelled to the ground and several of their other batteries were silenced, along with one of their magazines being blown up. This gave a great encouragement and we were expecting to receive an order to storm the town, as their fire had ceased entirely when the explosion took place, but it was only a moment's duration when they again opened fire upon us as quick as ever and were answered as promptly by us.

A short time after the occurrence just named took

place, just such another took place in the French lines by which they lost nearly 500 men, killed and wounded, and were unable to fire another gun for more than three days, which was a bad job for us as we had to bear the whole brunt of the enemy's fire while our allies were repairing their works, which had been damaged by the accident.

The Siege of Sebastopol by Adolphe Yvon (1855)

The fire was so rapid that, long before the evening, our magazines were emptied of all their ammunition and the fire from our batteries was slackened considerably for the want of it. The enemy, in the meantime, kept hammering away as hard as they could, while we could only give them a shot now and then until a supply of ammunition arrived from our main magazine, distant about 2 miles from the batteries. It was brought down in artillery wagons to the works, as near as possible. It was then conveyed to the magazine by the fatigues, who were employed in the trenches, and those men were constantly exposed to the enemy's fire.

At this time, evening was approaching fast, yet the fire from both sides, as we had now plenty of ammunition, was kept up with vigour. The total number of killed and wounded on the left attack was 75 rank and file and two officers, while the loss on the part of the enemy must have been very great as their trenches and batteries were alive with men. About 8 o'clock in the evening, we were relieved by a fresh party of the 4th Division, and glad we were to retire towards our camp after being exposed to the enemy's fire for upwards of 12 hours.

The Allied Commanders

The fire was kept up both day and night for the period of five days, when it ceased altogether on the part of the Allies, as it was plainly seen by the Allied Commanders that they could not make any impression on the enemy's works at the distance they were from them. As to storming the town, it was out of the question, so there was no alternative but to throw up fresh works considerably in advance of our present ones, which we soon set about doing.

8. THE BATTLE OF BALACLAVA: 25 OCT 1854

The first siege against Sebastopol closed on the 22nd October and, on the 25th of the same month, the Battle of Balaclava was fought.

It was about 8 o'clock in the morning when news reached the camp that the enemy had made a desperate attack on Balaclava and in great force. Their object was to take possession of the town where the whole of the British Army's stores lay. It was our weakest point, for there was only Cavalry, one regiment of Infantry, the 93rd Highlanders, and a few Artillery with about 14 or 15 guns. That was all the troops that were there to meet an army of 50,000 men[13] of the enemy.

When the enemy were seen to approach too close, every man available was ordered under arms, placed in as favourable position as circumstances would allow and waited patiently for the advance of the enemy, who were coming up in thousands. And no doubt they thought they would crush our little band that was drawn up on the heights to oppose them. But that little band was composed of Britain's sons, who would sooner die at their guns than yield one single inch to the overwhelming force that was coming against them.

Orders had been sent out to the front for reinforcements a distance of seven miles. At the same time the plains of Balaclava were filled with the dead and dying. Our Artillery, though few in number, had made fearful havoc in the enemy's ranks.

---

[13] Official numbers are around twenty-five thousand Russians

There was one battery mounted with 4 guns manned by the Turks and, after they had received a few shots from the enemy, they deserted it and it fell into the hands of the Cossacks.

As soon as our commanders saw that the battery was in possession of the foe and that they were preparing to turn our own guns upon us, the Cavalry was ordered to charge and retake it, and that fatal order was no sooner given than obeyed.

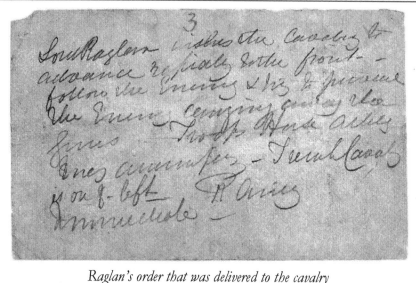

Raglan's order that was delivered to the cavalry

They did not number more than from six or eight hundred men, yet onwards they dashed amid a storm of shot and shell that was pouring in upon them from the enemy's guns, cutting their way through the ranks of the enemy's horses that were sent out to meet them, emptying scores of saddles, forcing their way up to their batteries and cutting down the gunners as they stood at their guns. Such effect had this charge that it threw the enemy into confusion. This was taken advantage of by our Artillery and Infantry, who forced volley after volley into their confused ranks, or masses, with such deadly effect that they fell in hundreds on the plains.

The Charge of the Light Brigade by William Simpson (1854)

By this time, a good support had arrived from the front and they lost no time in getting into battle, but it was not needed for the fight was over and the enemy was retiring from the bloodstained plains of Balaclava, leaving thousands[14] of their men dead or dying behind them.

Our loss was telling in the Infantry, but I am sorry to say the Artillery and Cavalry suffered severely, especially the cavalry, for there was no more than 200 of the brave fellows who returned from that fatal charge. The plain presented a fearful sight that evening where the Cavalry met in that deadly charge. The ground was torn up as though a plough had been drawn through it and the dead lay in heaps on the ground opposite the battery that was

---

[14] Though records vary slightly, the actual number of dead and wounded was hundreds, rather than thousands. Specifically around 600.

taken from the Turks in the early part of the day, and the courage and daring displayed in that deadly charge was never equalled by the same number of troops before.

This ended the Battle of Balaclava. The dead were interred that evening and the following day.

Cavalryman who survived the Charge of the Light Brigade

9. THE BATTLE OF INKERMAN: 5 NOVEMBER 1854

Very soon after this engagement, the troops that had laid so long on the ground at night, exposed to all weathers, had tents issued to them. And not before they wanted them, I can assure you, as the weather was getting very cold and the want of sufficient covering was felt very much by us, for we could plainly see that we should have to winter on the dreary heights of rock in front of Sebastopol.

November had now set in and, on the 5th of this month, was fought one of the bloodiest battles on record: that of Inkerman. The morning of that day was thick and hazy and, as heavy rains had visited the camps a day or two previous, inside and out it was a complete slough. Yet that did not prevent the enemy from endeavouring to take our camp by surprise.

About 4 o'clock in the morning they succeeded, although a thick fog covered the whole camp and made it difficult to discern anything at a distance, in getting into order of battle on our right flank. They threw several rounds of shot, shell and grape into the camps of our 2nd Division, who were posted there. The men of the Division had just returned off trench duty and some were preparing breakfast for themselves, others enjoying a short sleep, but they were soon roused by a rough salute from the enemy's guns ploughing up the ground and tearing the tents down about their ears - half of the poor fellows were naked under their blankets - killing and wounding several of the men and creating a great confusion amongst them. But this did not last long, for the firing no sooner began than the alarm spread through the camp that the enemy were upon us. Orders were given to stand to our arms and were obeyed as quick as given so that, in a short time, the whole of the troops capable of bearing arms were ready to aid and assist to the utmost in punishing the foe, who had so daringly entered our camps.

Setting for the Battle of Inkerman

The Russians were in great force, numbering at least 60,000 to 80,000 men and a numerous Artillery[15], while the British had no more 6,000 to keep that overwhelming force at bay, which they did for more than four hours, contending hand-to-hand with the enemy for that space of time. Nor was the British army at that time able to send them any assistance, as our hospitals were full with our

---

[15] The official number of Russians is 42,000 with 134 guns. British troops numbered 7,500 together with 8,200 French, with a total of 56 guns.

sick and wounded men. Yet every man that was able to stand under arms and was not on duty in the trenches were marched to the scene of action. Still, there were no more than about 8,000 British troops engaged through that day, yet they held their ground and, when their ammunition was all gone, they kept them at bay with the point of the bayonet until fresh supplies of ammunition were brought them.

The reinforcements who came up fell into the ranks without a murmur, to enjoy the share of the fight that their comrades had fought so well that day for the honour of Old England. They were received with a cheer and then rushed upon the foe to slay or die in defence of the Queen and Country. You may be sure by this time our ranks were fearfully thinned by the repeated charges of the enemy, and a great many of our officers had fallen while leading on their men to take a part in the game of life and death that was being played between us and the Russians on the heights of Inkerman.

We were mixed up with the enemy, advancing and retiring with the tide of battle and nothing but our bayonet to work with. So close were we mixed with the enemy that there was no other recourse but the point of bayonet or the butt of the firelock. And around us lay heaps of dead and dying, and the groans of the wounded would shock any person, no matter how strong in frame, and I really do believe that we should have had to retire before their superior numbers, had the enemy continued to pour in upon our little force, now reduced to nearly half of its small numbers.

At this critical moment, the heads of the French columns could be seen coming to our relief. This served to cheer us on to greater exertions. They were soon upon the field of fight and their presence was greeted with a good cheer that could be heard above the din of battle and, side-by-side, they rushed upon the foe with us and threw in their dense columns of Infantry. Withering volleys of musketry, aided with the heavy discharges of Artillery they brought with them, soon made a division in our favour, though the battle continued to rage as hard as ever - and for hours after, but it was not maintained all on the same ground, where they came up, as it was before. No, they were driven from one height to another and their numbers decreased every moment, for the French troops were all fresh and they took every advantage that offered itself. They gave no quarter and received none.

French soldiers in the Crimea

The battle had lasted now about eight hours and not less than 20,000 men lay dead or dying on the gory plains of Inkerman. It was about four o'clock in the evening before the enemy were finally driven from the field and the last gun was fired. They were pursued by the allies, who continued to thin the ranks by the quick discharges from the guns of the Artillery and the small arms of the Infantry, till night put a stop to the slaughter. The Russians are a brave foe and were drilled in field exercise, but the Briton still carries the conquering flags.

The dead and dying, friend and foe, officers and men, lay moaning all night where they fell the day before and the remnant of our little army returned to their camps, sick and weary from what they had witnessed that day.

As soon as daylight appeared the following morning, the survivors of that day's fight were ordered out to assist in placing their comrades, that had fallen that day, in their last homes on Earth and in conveying the wounded to where they could be taken care of and their sufferings attended to.

The field presented a most shocking sight. There could be seen in some parts of the field, where the contact has been more severe than another, a Frenchman and a Russian with their bayonets sheathed in each other's bodies. The same with the English and Russians. Both France and England lost, that day, some of as brave men as ever drew a sword in defence of their country. Among the slain was found the body of that brave Sir George Cathcart and several other officers, who fell that day to rise no more. The loss on the part of the allies was estimated at 8,000 men, that on the part of the enemy at 2,000.[16] I am

---

[16] Official numbers are 3,200 Russians killed, with a further 7,000 wounded, and 900 Allies dead with 3,700 wounded.

sure there could be not less, for they lay on the ground as thick in different places as bees around a beehive and were buried by the hundred in one hole, forming a grave. On the next day and the day after, the Russians were buried by themselves. The English and French likewise.

Aftermath of the Battle of Inkerman

10. WINTER: NOVEMBER 1854 - MARCH 1855

The British army was greatly reduced by these three engagements and the sickness that prevailed amongst the troops at this time. There was more than one half of the British army that had landed in the Crimea either dead or in the hospitals, so that the duty fell very heavy on the few that were left to perform it. And the winter had set in with all the inclemency attending such a season in this country.

British soldiers in winter dress

The rain continued to fall, intermingled with snow, for a period of forty days or more without ceasing little or much.

This month we felt the want of clothing and provisions very much. Still the duty had to be done and I have seen several of the men, when ordered out in the morning, with snow up to their middle, the water and mud of the clay soil of the camp reaching far above the ankle, with neither shoes nor stockings on their feet, or perhaps their shoes were frozen so hard that they could not put them on. In fact, you might see many men with their boots under their arms, endeavouring to thaw or soften them from the heat of their bodies so as to enable them to put them on their swollen and bleeding feet.

On the 14th of November, the camp was visited by a dreadful gale of wind such as I suppose no man scarcely ever saw before. There was not a tent or marquee in the whole camp left standing. The gale continued with heavy rain from daylight in the morning until late in the evening. We were exposed, the whole of that miserable day, to the inclemency of the weather, without food or clothing except what we had on our backs, and they were all saturated with rain. To make the matter better, the regiment was detailed for the duty of the trenches that night, without a particle of dry clothing upon us and nothing to eat except a few small pieces of wet biscuit, that was exposed to the rain all day, to serve for a meal, through a long and weary night's watch in the trenches, and under fire of the enemy.

Our poor comrades, that were lying ill in the hospital marquees, were unable to help themselves when the covering was torn from them and the marquees taken from over their heads by the rude blast of winds that swept over the camps. There the poor fellows lay entirely naked, for the blankets and rugs were blown into the air like so many paper kites. They were exposed like this the whole of the day, for it was impossible to erect any covering for them, or anyone else, during the time the gale lasted. There were no less than 14 men who died that day in the hospital from being exposed to the inclemency of the weather.

A wounded soldier

What made it worse for those men who were doing duty in the camps was this: out of ten or twelve men who slept in each tent, there would be perhaps six or eight of them on the hospitals' books, totally unable to help themselves with medicine or nourishment beyond the usual fare of biscuit and salt meat, which you will allow is not very tempting to a man half-dead. And this coarse food sometimes had to be eaten raw as there was no means of cooking it, for there was no fuel of any kind to be had except what could be gathered from the hillside or by digging up the roots of small bushes or picking up loose twigs that we might happen to meet in our paths as we walked about to and from the trenches. I have been for days together without once partaking of a warm meal, and all this time the works in the trenches are expected to go forward just as well as if the men were in comfortable quarters at some garrison town at home where they could have everything that would make toil and hardships, in a time like this, a pleasure. It was not so with us on the Crimea.

Money was of no use to us, because we could get nothing for it as there was no canteen or anything of the kind where you could purchase any little thing you wanted. For a long time after our arrival in front of Sebastopol, we could not get, either for love or money, a smoke of tobacco, which was as much wanted by the men, who were in the habit of using it, as anything else. I have heard men who had money offer to others, who had tobacco, 5, 10 and 15 shillings for a stick weighing about 2 oz, and you must be a great friend to get it then, not for the sake of the money, but it be to oblige the purchaser.

The Commissariat in the Crimea

The Commissariat supplied us sometimes with coffee and sugar, but there was more trouble in getting a fire ready to cook it than it was almost worth, as the coffee was served out to us in the berry (green) so that we had to roast it before we could do anything with it as regards cooking. When that was done, instead of putting it in a mill to grind it, we had to get a 32 pound shot and then place a few of the berries in a piece of rag (getting the rag where we could). If no rag could be got, get a flat stone and lay the berries on the stone and roll the shot over them until crushed enough for use or to our satisfaction (which was not hard to please at this time).

It would then go into the canteen or camp kettle to boil and, perhaps after going to all that trouble, just as it was ready for use, having planted ourselves on the ground to partake of it, it being perhaps the first warm meal that has entered our insides for 2 or 3 days, we would be called away upon duty to some other part of the camp. If so, we must either leave it behind or carry it in our hands and partake of it as we go, to assist to wash down a portion of the hard biscuit into our stomachs.

At this part of the play we were almost naked, with scarcely a shoe to our feet or a rag to our backs, and if we had any in possession, we had no time or soap to wash them with. As for shaving or washing, it was not thought of at this time scarcely at all. If a man got an opportunity of washing his hands and face once in two or three days, he would boast of it for nearly a week afterwards. As that was the case, we were all, from the Generals down to the private soldiers, covered with vermin through not having time to keep our person and clothes clean.

During this time, the work in front of the enemy had

progressed rapidly. Our second trench, with three new batteries, was finished and a third one opened at a distance of 200 yards in front of the second, which brought us within half a mile of the enemy's works. They were ready to open fire a second time.

Time was rolling on and we were in possession of a portion of winter clothing that had been brought from Balaclava and issued to the troops, and much it was required, for we had scarcely a remnant of the clothing in possession that we landed in the Crimea with. It would have astonished anyone, had they seen us parading for duty, as a more ragged group could never meet together than we were at this time of the year. You would see some of us with an old great coat, some perhaps with their shirts off, the sleeves tied close to our arms, with a piece of sacking that we got from the Commissariat, made to resemble gaiters or perhaps trousers, tied round our bodies and legs with a plentiful supply of rope, yarn or any that would answer the purpose of fastening them to us. In fact no one could have told what we were, as we had no appearance of British soldiers at all, except by our accoutrements, for we were more like Tartars, who have as many rags and strings about them as would make a fortune for any old bone and rag gatherer in England if they had hold of them. But still we dare not attempt to discard our old friends (the rags) until we had got a complete suit to replace them with.

This was the way we were dressed the first winter on the Crimea, which was the death of hundreds of our brave comrades and caused others to lose their legs, toes and fingers through being frostbitten. But the winter passed rapidly away, and a prospect of fine weather soon set in as we were now in the month of March, and the enemy now and then paid us a visit in the shape of a sortie on our works, which now began to look formidable. And the men appeared to be anxiously looking forward for the time when they might again speak to Jonny Ruse[17], through the iron throats of our bristling cannon.

Cannons ready for action

---

[17] This appears to be a term, similar to 'Johnny Bono', referring to the Russians.

11. THE SIEGE OF SEBASTOPOL CONTINUES: APRIL - AUGUST 1855

Nor did they wait long, for, on the 9th of April, being Easter Monday, though the rain was descending in torrents so that every man who was not on duty was obliged to keep inside his tent, at about 5 o'clock in the morning, we were suddenly startled by the heavy booming of cannon. We thought the enemy was going to stir us up with another Inkerman, but our fears in that respect were groundless. But, on going to the rise of the hill overlooking the town of Sebastopol, we saw with delight that the whole of the allied guns had opened once more their mouths and were throwing in hard words, in the shape of shot and shell, into the enemy's works. We thought, surely, that we should be able to bring the enemy to subjection during the siege, but we were again disappointed, and our Authorities saw that we were yet too far away and that our shot and shell made little or no impression on the earthen works that the enemy's batteries were composed of. So this siege lasted only four days, just to let the enemy know that we were not all dead or asleep. When the firing ceased the second time, the amount of casualties were very trifling; during the continuation of the siege, not more than forty men were killed and about the same number wounded.

So there was nothing for it but to creep as close to the enemy's works as possible, which we did by throwing up new works in front of those already erected. We were kept constantly at work either in the trenches or making roads about our camp. As the fine weather had set in and the men began to recover from the severe effect of the winter, everything began to wear a more cheerful appearance. We could now find a little time to attend to our own wants, better than we could a few months ago. And, there being a sufficient quantity of clothing in the store for our use, we were now both clean and comfortable, as far as war will comfort anyone. And along with that we had the means of purchasing different articles such as groceries and a drop of Old Tom[18] or rum, and tobacco was getting cheap, which is the soldier's friend on the trenches of a cold night. Our rations were good, together with the means of cooking them, and we were as happy as princes, compared to what we were during the winter months. So if we had to work hard, we did not think anything about it.

The camp of the 3rd Division

The enemy never gave us a call, but we were always ready to receive them and they never left us without getting a few pills from the tubes of our rifles that they

---

[18] The slang name for Gin.

found hard to digest. From the opening of the first siege to the close of the second occupied six months, and this time the regiment was scarcely able to furnish men for the duty required of them. The 38th regiment left England with 900 hundred Bayonet and, at this time, there was not more than 350 men that came out with us left in the regiment to do duty. This will serve to show you how, in the space of twelve months, our numbers decreased. Yet our ranks were nearly filled up to their usual strength by drafts coming out from the depots at home.

The 38th Regiment (Richard Barnham's in there somewhere!)

On the 5th June, the third siege opened on the enemy's works and continued for two days, when one of the principle batteries was taken from them by the French storming it on the right attack - the name of the Fort they took was the Mamelon - after an hour's hard fighting, although the enemy strove hard to dislodge their daring foe and gain possession of what they had lost. After repeated attacks made by them to do so, they were forced to retire and still leave it in the hands of the allies.

On the same day, the English made an attack on the rifle pits or what was afterwards termed the Quarries. This they did under a very heavy fire from the Great Redan and other batteries that could bring their guns to bear upon us. The Mamelon was taken almost without a struggle. Not so with the Quarries, for we met with a desperate and determined resistance.

Three times did the British troops rush to the assault and were driven back. Our guns in the batteries threw into the enemy fearful discharges of shot and shell, which shook the earth around us and scores lost their lives in that brief and deadly struggle. Notwithstanding the disadvantage of our position to that of the enemy, we succeeded with great loss in our undertaking, and drove the enemy to seek shelter in the Redan and Malakoff batteries. Although the enemy made more than one effort to retake the place, they found it in vain, for they never made the attempt but that it cost them many valuable lives. This was the first time the Allies had made an attack on any of their works and it proved successful and beneficial to us, as it enabled us to throw in a good crossfire into their works and their guns, which galled them more and more. These Quarries, in a short time, proved one of the largest batteries we had in possession. We lost about 350 men while taking them. This affair took place on the 7th of June 1855.

From this period up to the 18th of June, we were employed in filling our magazines and making the works in the trenches as strong as possible and, in addition to our other batteries, we erected a battery of eleven mortars on the right of the third parallel adjoining the Woronzoff

Road[19], which did great execution on the town when the Artillery men received the order to destroy it.

The Woronzoff Road

At this period of the siege, the troops were only relieved every twenty-four hours and any person seeing them there would have been astonished to see with what indifference they looked upon the shot and shell that was flying about them. We used to play all kinds of games. Some could be seen playing cards, others tossing halfpence, others throwing the shot with his comrade to see who could throw it the furthest, while every now and then a shot or shell could be seen high in the air, thrown by the enemy. This would cause them to cease, for a time, the game they were at to allow this messenger of death to alight and burst, while they would be hid under the

---

[19] This road ran from Sebastopol to the harbour at Balaclava.

embankment of the trench until such time as the fragments of the shell had passed over them. Then they would spring up again, and continue their games, as unconcerned as if there was no danger in the flying and bursting of those death-dealing shells. At another part of the works could be seen a group of attentive listeners to a newspaper that was being read by a comrade soldier, who received it from some kind friend or relative at home. For I assure you that a newspaper was highly prized by the soldiers in the Crimea. Such was the way we generally used to employ ourselves in the trenches; that is, when the enemy did not find us work of a rougher nature to employ our time upon, which they seldom did in the daytime, and at night there was always a careful watch set to guard against surprise.

Soldiers relaxing between duties

All things continued to go on in this manner with little or no attention, unless it was repelling a sortie made upon us now and then by the enemy, just by way of keeping our hand in practice, until the 16th June, when the 4th siege was opened by the allies pouring into the enemy's works a tremendous fire from every battery they had in their possession, which could not be less than 3 or 4 hundred guns, beside mortar and rocket battery, which wasn't a few I can assure you. Nor did the Russians forget to give us as good as we sent. This was carried on, night and day, on both sides and, during this siege, the Allied Commanders took it into their heads to have a slap at the town.

The morning of the 18th was the day appointed for the business to be done. The Regiments that paraded belonging to the 3rd Division for that purpose were the 9th, 18th, 28th, 38th[20] and 44th Regiments. It was about one o'clock in the morning when the troops left the camps and proceeded towards the intended place of attack, commanded by Brigadier General Eyre. On the day previous to the attack, there were men selected from the different regiments composing a Brigade. As a forlorn hope, their object was to drive the enemy from the rifle posts, as there were several in the way of our advance, and take possession themselves. This party numbered about 700 men and they met with a determined resistance from the enemy, who knew that if they lost that position they could not prevent us getting into the cemetery and thence perhaps into the town itself.

As the English were to attack both the Redan and the cemetery, while the French on the right made an attack on

---

[20] That being Richard's regiment.

the Malakoff, we were to advance under cover of our own guns, which were melodiously playing and endeavouring to clear the way in front of us.

At a given signal from the French, the Malakoff and Redan was to be attacked at once. The signal was to be a blue rocket thrown into the air.

By this time our sharpshooters had got into the cemetery and the Brigade was steadily advancing towards the scene of action, and I do not know whether the enemy had got notice of our approach or not, but this I know, they were ready to receive us. No sooner had the heads of our columns shown themselves than they opened one of the most destructive fires that ever anyone witnessed. So close and deadly was the fire thus thrown into our ranks that is was found impossible to advance in anything like battle array. We were accordingly ordered to get under cover, the best way we could, from the fearful discharges of grape and canister that was being thrown into our ranks and mowing down our men by dozens.

At this time we had a flat piece of ground of about 400 yards, that lay between the cemetery and the entrance to the town, to cross before we could get under cover at all. We thought it was better to cross this flat than remain where we were to be shot like cats and dogs and not having a chance to return the compliment. Directly in front of us stood several houses, which it was now our object to reach as they were the only cover that was to be seen at that time. To reach this cover of houses, we had to encounter the fire from the whole of the Batteries that could bring their guns to bear upon us. It was a dreadful trial to get over this flat. It was there that hundreds of our men fell while endeavouring to get to some place that would shelter them from the deadly fire of the enemy and that would enable them to try the effect of our own guns upon the enemy and their works. We succeeded at length in getting under cover of those houses with the loss of about half our men.

The Great Redan battery after its defeat

During the time we had been getting to this place, the signal had been given by the French to attack the Redan, which was accordingly done by the troops on the right attack. But I am sorry to say that, after a most desperate attempt made by us to get possession of it, we had to retire with heavy losses. More than once or twice did the British troops succeed in getting into the enemy's works, but found it impossible to hold them, so great was the force brought to oppose us.

While we were making these desperate and bloody attempts on the Redan, the French took the advantage -

while the enemy were engaged with us at the Redan - to make the assault on the Malakoff. They did this at the time when nothing could be seen for smoke nor anything could be heard for the roaring of the cannon that was belching forth their messengers of death and destruction all around. The enemy did not expect an attack on that part of their territories, but the French made the attack at the proper time to the minute and succeeded in getting possession and holding it for a long time. But, like ourselves, they had to retire from it with a loss of about 4,000 men[21], so that the whole attack from right to left proved a failure, except what the Brigade of the 3rd Division took at the commencement and kept: that being the graveyard or cemetery. This they held the whole day and, when the enemy saw they could not drive them from it, they turned their guns upon the houses and levelled them to the ground. Those men who were in the cemetery were not released from that position until 10 o'clock at night. They had been there in the position since about half past four a.m. under a very heavy fire from all around us.

When it got sufficiently dark and the fire on both sides, after such a day's bloodshed, had almost ceased, we began as well as we could to remove the wounded to a place of greater security and to retire towards our camps, very much fatigued from such a day's work as we had gone through and the way we had been defeated that day for the first time on the Crimea. Our own loss in the 38th Regiment was one officer killed and seven wounded. The number of non-commanding officers and privates killed

---

[21] Officially there were 3,500 French casualtles.

and wounded on that day was 350[22].

The trenches around the Malakoff

On the next day, a flag of truce was hoisted on both sides for the purpose of burying the dead and removing the wounded that had been left on the field all night. It took us the chief part of the day to perform this sad duty and, during the time we were digging the graves for the remains of our departed comrades, the Russians left their works and mingled with us, talking in a most friendly manner, if we could only have understood them. There they were looking at us putting the poor fellows, who had been slain the day before, into the yawning grave that was made to receive them. We shook hands with some and even exchanged biscuit for some liquor they had with them called Raki[23]. They thought our food very white, and so it was to what theirs was, for they all eat linseed bread, quite

---

[22] Actually 150 according to the casualty lists.

[23] Rakı was a popular alcoholic drink of the Ottoman Emprie, flavoured with aniseed, similar to Ouzo.

black, for all the world like oil-cake. This they were doing, with all the good nature in the world, and us the same. And perhaps in less than 2 hours after this, if we met together, we would thrust the bayonet through each other's bodies. Such is war.

This defeat of the British troops on the 18th June made us feel rather downhearted for a time, and we thought we should never get into the town at all. Yet we knew, if courage and perseverance could do anything, we had plenty of that amongst us to overcome all obstacles.

From the 18th June to the 28th of that month, the duties of camp went on the same as usual and, on the 28th, the death of our Commander-in-Chief took place (Lord Raglan). He was a brave and considerate General. His death was regretted by all the British army.

On the 12th of August, the fifth siege opened on Sebastopol and every time the siege opened there were always more guns added to the numbers, though the siege lasted only a few days at a time, owing to our not being close enough to their works.

On the 16th August, the sixth siege opened and continued their fire more or less up to the end of that month, when we had approached as near to their works as it was possible for us to go.

12. THE FALL OF SEBASTOPOL: SEPTEMBER 1855

On the evening of the 7th of September, the Regiment formed the guard for the trenches. Everything bore the silence of the grave as we marched down to the works and for a considerable time afterwards, when, all at once, the silence of the night was broken by a salvo from the French and English Batteries that shook the earth for miles around us. And that destructive fire was all directed on the town of Sebastopol. There was no less than 600 guns and mortars playing at one time on that devoted place - a place which had cost so many of the courageous soldiers of the British army to get to the position we had held in front of it.

Mortar Battery (on a slow day)

On the morning of the 8th, the whole of the allied Army was under arms, ready to be sent to any part of the field that their presence might be required. And the first that was thrown from our Batteries into the works of the enemy and Sebastopol was truly terrifying, for the enemy could not stand to work their guns nor stay in their works at all. There was not a house in the town but what was injured more or less by our shot and shell.

It was about 9 o'clock in the morning that that attack was made by the English and French on those two formidable forts, the Redan and Malakoff. The French succeeded in getting into the Malakoff and took possession of it.

The French attack on the Malakoff by William Simpson (1855)

The French came on them so sudden that they flew from the Malakoff and reinforced their men in the Redan with several thousand men from the aforesaid fort, just at the time when our light divisions were ordered to attack it.

Yet they did not prevent our British from dashing to it and endeavouring to achieve a conquest superior to that which our brave Allies had so easily obtained. But it was not to be. For, what with the powerful reinforcements they had received and the determined resistance they made, for they well knew that, if the French could get the opportunity of turning the guns that were in the Malakoff onto the town and at the back of the Redan, they would soon lose all the men that were in it. So, as it was a game that every man inside their fort was interested in, they were determined to hold out as long as the men were capable of bearing arms against us. And hold it they did, in spite of the desperate attempt that was made by the British troops to drive them from it. Three times over did they rush to the assault and were driven back, with great loss, although they succeeded in getting into it, but could not stop there, so great was the force they had to contend with. Inside, the men fell by scores, by endeavouring to hold the ground they had fought so hard to obtain. It was a long and bloody struggle, as our dead and dying that lay in heaps around us and all round the fort could testify. But still we could not help or assist them at that time. Fight as desperately as we would, it appeared to be for no good purpose. Yet did our men continue this unequal contest til near sunset in the evening, when a recall was sounded for the troops to retire into their own works, which they did, leaving hundreds of their comrades either dead or dying in front of the great Redan. But we were determined not to be beaten, but to have Sebastopol. We would, if it cost us another army to come from England.

This was the intention of the Allied Commanders. So another attack was to have taken place at 8 o'clock the following morning. And as the force that was sent to the attack the day before could not subdue it, the 3rd and 4th Divisions were ordered to attack it at the above time, each division numbering 11 Regiments, each Regiment about 850 men, leaving with all about 19,700 men. But, long before the time appointed, the enemy had abandoned the South side of the town altogether, sinking their shipping in different parts of the harbour to blockade our ships from making their way to the mouth of the harbour during the night. And as they retired from their works, they blew up their magazines, destroying their fortifications by spiking their guns and setting fire to their dwellings and destroying everything they could to prevent them falling into the hands of the Allies.

The ruins of Sebastopol, seen from the Malakoff

It was not more than half an hour after the intelligence arrived to the camps that the town was abandoned, when hundreds of soldiers, both French and English, could be seen making their way into the enemy's city, that stronghold that had placed the Allied Armies so long at defiance. There we were, all inside at last, running from house to house, over heaps of dead and dying, in search of plunder. Nor did we look long, for there was plenty to be had for carrying away. Nor was it long afterwards before they could be seen coming back to their camps loaded, some with a pig on his back, others galloping away on horses, others leading away cows and bullocks and in fact all kinds of cattle, others taking furniture of the dearest description. And you may depend, there was not a house in the town but what was searched by both English and French. But the English were made to leave them down as soon as they got clear of the town and, the French taking them up and carrying them away from us with no one to prevent them, the English thought it very hard, after looking at the town so long and fighting to get into it, and would not be allowed to benefit themselves by the plunder as well as the French.

A narrow valley near Sevastopol which was in range of the Russian guns. British soldiers were paid a few pence for each cannonball they retrieved.

13. THE END OF THE CAMPAIGN: OCTOBER 1855 - JULY 1856

After the fall of the town, the trench duty ceased so that we had no more hardships of that kind to suffer. In fact, we had nothing to do but guard duties and field practice. We had a great number of sentinels around that part of the town belonging to us.

In the month of October, parties from each regiment were employed in making roads from Sebastopol to Balaclava for the purpose of conveying what property fell into our hands in the town of Balaclava, previous to its being shipped for England. This employment continued for about two months, when the material for erecting huts for the troops had arrived from England. So, while one part of the army were employed in making roads, the other part were employed in carrying up to their camps their huts and putting them together. This was done in the depth of winter and, you may be sure, this duty was very fatiguing, but we thought nothing of it as it was for our own benefit. It was cheerfully done, but the army's huts were not all up until the month of February, so that the Winter of 1855 passed away with Balaclava fatigues and Sebastopol guards and duties.

In the month of November, a dreadful explosion took place at the right siege train. A French Magazine, containing about 200 tons of gunpowder beside live shell and other combustible matter, blew up and, this being close to one of the British magazines, it ignited likewise, and was the cause of a great many deaths and wounds. The shot, shell and fragments of beams of the huts were strewed all over the camps for a mile or two around the place of misfortune. And several men who were lying sick in the hospitals close at hand were killed and wounded, and at the same time, the poor men were all sick, under medical attendance.

On the 3rd of March, an Armistice was entered into with the Russians by the Allied Commanders, and hostilities ceased on both sides for one month. During this truce, we had an opportunity of seeing some of the Russians of all sexes, who had used to come to our lines for the purpose of exchanging anything we may have in our possession to exchange with them as trophies.

During this month, very strong parties were employed in pulling down houses in Sebastopol and carrying the wood to the camps for fuel. The beautiful and expensive docks were destroyed, not one stone was left standing upon another, and along with this the whole of the stores, such as shot and shell, guns, mortars and everything belonging to the Allies, was cleared away and carried to Balaclava, ready for to be shipped, if necessary, so that Sebastopol was nothing but a mass of ruins from right to left.

On the 30th of March, peace was signed at Paris between the four great powers, which may depend was received with much joy by everyone at home and abroad, and by none more than the soldiers in the Crimea, as every man could look forward for a speedy return to England, to his family and friends, after an absence of nearly two years and a half, under such sufferings and hardships as no army in the world ever experienced before.

After peace being proclaimed, the last fatigue the

Gathering for the Treaty of Paris

British troops performed in front of Sebastopol was collecting the whole of the shot that the enemy threw at us during the sieges, which was no few. You would actually think that it looked like a field in which some potatoes had been dug up and left on the top of the ground. They lay so thick and many times we fell over them going to and fro from the trenches in the dark winter nights.

In the month of May, the Regiments, after leaving their camps in a clean and good order, were removed to Balaclava to assist in putting the stores - at that place there was an immense quantity of every description - on board ship for further conveyance to England. In this month, the troops were leaving the Crimea and proceeding to the different stations allotted for them daily, and with great spirits and light hearts, thinking to leave that place where so many thousands were left behind.

In the month of April, the whole of the British army was reviewed by the Russian Commander General Lüders, who expressed himself to be highly satisfied with our appearance and discipline. It was a noble sight. I suppose there was not a man in the whole army ever saw so much of a staff together in their lives. There were English, French, Turkish, Sardinian, Polish and Russian Commanders. Our army was but small in numbers at this time, but all were in good condition and well in health, ready for any army they might meet. There we stood, proud of ourselves and our Country, a pride that the countless hoards of Russians could not rob us of.

Ships in the Balaclava Harbour

On the 20th of June 1856, we were under order to hold ourselves in readiness to proceed to Old England, again on HMS Caesar, and, you may be sure, we were looking daily for the vessel to come into the harbour and to receive the order to embark, which we did on the 26th of June. We embarked at Balaclava on board the aforesaid vessel and left that place, which we suffered so much in and left so many of our comrades behind us. And after a pleasant voyage of 23 days' duration, we landed at Portsmouth on the 22nd of July, without any incident, at the same place we had embarked 2 or 3 years before.

The Regiment did not stay in Portsmouth, but proceeded to the railway station at Landport, at which place we remained for an hour and then proceeded to Aldershot camp, at which place we remained for a month, where we had plenty of drill and general field days to contend with.

Any person would have thought that, after undergoing so many dangers and hardships as the British army had done through the campaign, that they would have got a little time allowed to recover themselves a bit and been put into some comfortable quarters or other that would have enabled us to do so. But the authorities at home thought different, for as the soldiers were no longer required in the field, the cheerless canvas tent that creates diseases and filth of all kinds was quite good enough for us. And we all thought it was a poor reception after coming to our native country after so severe an absence.

During our stay at Aldershot, the Regiment were inspected by the Queen, who gave orders that all the men who went out with the Regiment and came home with it were to be drawn up into line that she may see how many there were that had been spared to tread once more on the land that gave them birth, which was accordingly done. The number that was left out of 950 Bayonet men, that being the strength of the regiment when it left the shores of old England on the 26th April 1854, the total number left for inspection of Her Majesty was 130, all ranks.

Photo of Queen Victoria taken in 1854

After the inspection, the regiment left Aldershot en route for Ireland. We reached Dublin on the morning of the 24th of August and then proceeded to the Camp Curragh, situated in the county Kildare, where we are at present stationed, and almost in as great an inconvenience as in the Crimea, as regards going for a walk to town, for we are on a wild plain.

I now bid my readers, whoever they may be, goodbye, hoping I may never have the occasion to pen such likes again, under such circumstances. I remain still an old campaigner.

Richard Barnham
Light Company
38th Regiment
Camp Curragh
Ireland

P.S. Whoever reads these passages must recollect they were written in the bustle and confusion of the Campaign and at no regular periods.

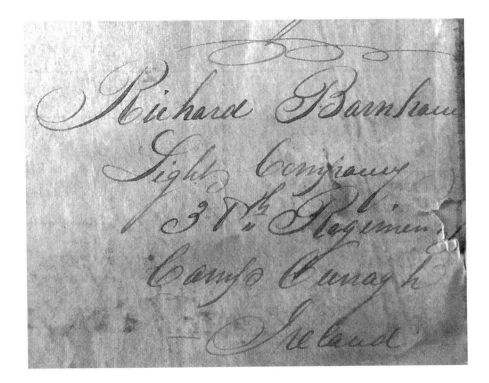

APPENDIX I: A LETTER FROM MALTA

The following letter was written by Richard Barnham to his parents, Richard and Mary, while on the island of Malta during the 38th Regiment's voyage to the Crimea:

Malta, May 9th 1854.
War time.

Dear Father and Mother,

I'm taking the pleasure of writing a few more lines to you, hoping to find you all in good health as, thanks be to God for it, I am at present. I sent you a letter as late as I possibly could before I left old England's shore. We expected to go on board of the ship that night we left Woolwich - on the 25th of April - but after marching and by going on train, we got into Portsmouth that night, and stopped there that night. We were played away from Woolwich with 2 bands of the Royal Artillery and the Marines, and we were cheered by the whole inhabitants of the town. They played us about 6 or 7 miles to the station at New Cross and then they left us. The whole of the inhabitants in that place was out to cheer us and the two bands as they left us, and then we parted and as soon as we got into Portsmouth there were two more bands to meet us to play us to our barracks where we stopped that night and the cheering was more than at Woolwich on account of us laying there before. The two bands that met us were the 79th Highlanders and the Rifle Brigade. We marched from the barracks to the dockyard about 3 o'clock on the evening of the 26th and went on board of the ship called the Megaera, a Man-of-War Screw Steamer. We stopped in harbour that night and on the 27th at about noon we started to sea. The wind was not fair so we started by steam and had a three-quarter breeze for three days and we sailed about 9 or 10 knots an hour, and on the 30th of the month, on Sunday, the time we were at Prayers, the wind shifted to a side breeze and we went only an hour. We saw neither a ship nor land from the time we left the Isle of White until the 30th. We met one, a small brig going to where we left.

I forgot to mention to you before about the other part of the Regiment. They left Chatham on the 24th of April in the Melbourne to go to the same place as us. They started a day and a night before us. The band is on board the Melbourne and Barrett is with them. On the night of the 30th of April, as we were going across the Bay of Biscay we saw two or three more ships and likewise about a half dozen very large whales blowing about the water. We still kept a pretty good breeze but we were obliged to keep up the steam too. It was rather a calm sea until the night of the 30th of May, when a very heavy gale came over. I was one that was on Watch that night. We had about 6 or 7 squalls came over us. We were putting up sails and taking them down all the night, and soon as we put them up, the wind came all in a sudden and we thought the ship was going to turn over several times. The sails flew in all directions and the masts were cracking, but in the morning about 5 o'clock it dropped and was pretty fair, so we took down the sails and put on the steam again.

About 7 o'clock on the 2nd of the month we were on the coast of Spain and, at about 10 or 11 o'clock, we saw land and we sailed close to the mountains and rocks all day. We passed a lighthouse on the mountains and the ships were beginning to come past us by dozens. On the evening of the 2nd we passed Portugal and still kept up our steam, and later in the evening we passed a mountain called the St Vincent and we saw no more land til the next day, at about 6 o'clock.

On the evening of the 3rd, it commenced raining very hard. It's uncomfortable on land but it's worse on board of ship by a great deal and it still kept on til the morning of the 4th. About 7 o'clock in the evening of the 3rd, we passed a very large fortification garrisoned by the Spaniards. We saw the Spanish soldiers on sentry as we passed by and on the morning of the 4th we sailed into what is called the gut of Gibraltar. It's about 20 or 30 miles from the Rock of Gibraltar. One side of the gut is Spain and the other barbarous. On both sides are rocks and mountains all over it. It looks to be all a wild country and, about 9 o'clock, we sailed past the rock of Gibraltar and it's a very nice place. It's supposed to be one of largest forts in the world. It's full of these short-tailed monkeys, there is many a thousand of them.

The wind was still fair for us, we had no steam on for two or three days, all the time we were in the gut. We saw a place called Tangiers, it is fortified by the barbarians, and then we left land again in the wide ocean and nothing could be seen, only the clouds and water, except our own ship. We had nice, fine weather. The weather is very hot now and was from the time we came into the gut. About 2 days after being on board, when the ship began to roll and rock, the whole of the Regiment that was on board of the ship was very much seasick and some were worse than others. I was very sick myself for 2 days. It's ten times worse than a drunken sickness. The whole of us was lying about on the decks like sheep and spewing all over one another and did not seem to care what became of us. But about the 5th day we were alright and, thanks be to God, I am as well as ever again. We still kept up all our sail till we sailed into the Mediterranean sea and then on the 5th we caught sight of land again on our right. It was the coast of Africa and we still kept sight of it till the 7th and then left it again.

On the morning of the 6th, the wind dropped and we had a calm sea. You could scarcely see the sea move at all, so we got up the steam again and travelled on. On the morning of the 7th we passed a transport ship which had onboard some Artillery. She was just moving and that's all. She started about 14 days before us and we've left her behind now about 6 days, that shows we have some benefit by coming on a steam ship. The climate still gets hotter, it's like being in an oven. By the time we come back we will be as dark as a black man. On the day of the 8th, we passed an Island called [Pantelleria] and on the 9th we passed another called [Gozo] and then the next was Malta, where we are now taking in coal for the remainder of the voyage. We do not know how long we are going to stop there.

You need not write til you hear from me again. So no more at present from your son,

Richard Barnham
No. 3041, No.3 Company, 38th Regiment
On the sea on board of the Megaera, 9th May, war time.

God Bless you all.

P.S. [This letter] was overweight so I was obliged to halve it.

APPENDIX II: 'RICHARD BARNHAM' BY MARION RUSSELL

The following text was written by Marion Russell (Richard Barnham's great-granddaughter):

Richard Barnham of Leeds had a distinguished military career. He fought in the Crimea War, 1853-56, when England and France joined Turkey to fight the Russians on the shores of the Black Sea. Richard fought in the battles at Alma, Inkerman and Sebastopol. What we remember best about this long-ago war, perhaps, are "The Charge of the Light Brigade", immortalised by Lord Tennyson's poem, and the exploits of that very famous nurse, Florence Nightingale.

Richard also fought in the Indian Mutiny, where he was one of the relieving troops at Lucknow.

Florence Nightingale

During his military campaigns he wrote a diary describing scenes on the battlefields and telling of the hardships suffered by the troops. It is remarkable that he could write and read! In the 1850s, many people were illiterate, because the Education Act, which established Elementary Education, was not passed until 1870. This diary can be seen in the Military Museum at Leeds, to which it was donated. Some members of the family have copies of it.

As a soldier, Richard would have worn a red coat with white or blue trousers and a tall cap called a shako. Around his waist would be a belt to hold bullets and diagonally across his body would be white belts for his water bottle at one side and his bayonet at the other.

Foot soldiers were armed with a rifle, which was muzzle loaded. The soldier bit off the end of a paper cartridge, poured the gunpowder down the barrel and rammed home the wad and the bullet. For charging the enemy, and for all close fighting, the bayonet was fixed to the rifle and used like a lance. The cavalry, known as dragoons and hussars, wore even more handsome uniforms. What bright targets they presented to the enemy! These cavalrymen, armed with lances, sabres and long pistols called carbines, took part in the Charge of the Light Brigade.

The cannon were known as field guns or artillery. They fired grape shot against troops, and canon balls against forts and buildings. These balls tore holes in walls, but did not explode like modern shells. Our British cannon were not successful in knocking down the strong walls of Sebastopol during the siege of that city. (Very naughtily, I get a funny mental picture of the poor gunners firing away at the walls, whilst the cannon balls bound off as if there were playing a game of squash! But war in those days was no topic for humour, and is even less so now).

Richard served firstly with the 38th Staffordshire Regiment, and then with the Leeds Rifles, a volunteer company of which he was an instructor. He represented the 38th Staffordshires as one of the bodyguard to the Prince of Wales, later King Edward VII, when he married Princess Alexandra of Denmark in 1863. Richard also fought in the Indian Mutiny, 1857-1858, and was one of the relieving troops at Lucknow.

Richard Barnham's Regimental Badge

After his time in the army, he acted as Mace Bearer to the Sheriff of Leeds and no doubt he would carry out his duties at important official occasions in a smart, soldierly manner.

His diary is devoted to military matters and gives few details of himself, his age, home background etc. I would assume that when he was soldiering abroad he was a young, unmarried man, and that he married Bessie and had 10 children at a later date. He reared no soldiers to follow in his footsteps, however; 8 of the 10 children were girls! His sons, William (my grandfather) and Francis, showed signs of their military upbringing however, both in their upright bearing and ability to assume command.

My grandfather was the proud owner of many trophies won by his father. I can well remember with what pride he showed me, and the other grandchildren, Richard's medals mounted on red velvet and in a heavy gilt frame. One medal was received from King Albert of the Belgians. One very rare possession was an Indian coin in use before Britain took over the mintage. I have a metal toe ring which Indian women wore on the big toe to indicate married state. Richard brought back this ring amongst his souvenirs in 1857, and also an ivory teething ring.

On the death of my grandfather, the framed medals, now worth a lot of money, were passed on to my cousin, Arthur Barnham, who was then a sailor fighting in the Second World War. (Artie, as we always called him, was the third son of Arthur, my grandfather's eldest son). When Artie died, his wife, Kathleen, kept them for a number of years and then passed them on to another cousin, William (Bill), son of my grandfather's second son, William (Willy).

Richard Barnham was one of the "Soldiers of the Queen". During Victoria's reign, the British Empire expanded until it could be hailed as an empire "on which the sun never sets". Credit for this magnificent achievement rested in large measure with the valorous armies of Britain and her colonies, the men of whom Victoria wrote, 'I am so fond of my dear soldiers... and so proud of them!'

APPENDIX III: AN EXCERPT FROM THE ORIGINAL JOURNAL

The following 10 pages are images taken of Richard Barnham's journal during Phin Hall's visit to the Staffordshire Regiment Museum in May 2015.

The complete diary can be viewed on the Lundarien Press website: *www.lundarienpress.com*

31th Regiment

Passages on the Crimean War.

The 31th Regiment left the shores of Old England at
Portsmouth on the 27th day of April in the Year of
our Lord 1854. For the seat of War in the East.
In the seventh days sail we sighted that strongholse
Gibralter where we had some splended Views of the
Spanish Coasts and other shores on our way to Malta
which noted place we reached on the Eleventh day
on leaving the shores of England.
We cast Anchor for a few hours while we watered
and coaled, the Harbour and Town was well
fortified and offered a safe Anchorage for Vessels of
the largest size which should happen to put in
there. As regards the Town it appeared as far as I
was able to judge from Board of Ship to be clean
and neatly laid out according to the custom and
manner of the people.
After getting a sufficient supply of Water, Fuel,
Provisions, and other articles, necessary for the troops
on board we got under weigh for the shores of
Turkey, nothing of importance occured during our
passage up from Malta to Gilipoli which place
we reached in safety and without any accident
on the 16th of May 1854.
We cast anchor in the Harbour of Gilipole close to a
Turkish Vessel of war where I witnessed a scene
that took place on that Vessel it was a scene that
not only astonished me, but every one that beheld
it it being at this time near Sun set, and as we
were in a strange Country, Our deck being crowded
with men, and each man eager to see and hear
what was going on around him the scene took
place that I am about to describe
The Sun at this time had nearly dispeared and the
shades of night began to throw her sable mantle over
the face of Nature When we were suddenly startled
by a deafening cheer from Jonny Bons as they
were termed by the Allies (Our Turkish Comrades)
we were supprised to see them one and all prostrate
themselves on the Vessels deck with their hands received
above their heads, After remaining in that position for
some time they rose on their knees, and still kept

to us to go through a form of Prayer bowing
frequently to the deck of the Vessel. After the Sun had
finally disappeared they sprang to there feet and cheered
again most lustily, we were a long time before we could
make out what they were doing, but we afterwards
learn, to that it was there Custom to pay homage to
the Sun when setting

We disembarked the following morning, this being the
17th day of May in the same year, And Marched on to
the Town of Gilipoli, if a Town it can be called for it
was nothing but a wretched collection of Huts and cabins
roughly thrown together and of the worst material some
were built with clay, others with wood, and the
remainder with a composition of clay, stone mud
and any thing else they could lay there hands on
to secure a temporay shelter from the rain and
heavy dews, to which the Country is subject &
As regards the streets and passages which led through
the Town of Gilipoli, they were in a most filthy
and dirty condition the streets were narrow and
strewed with all kinds of Rubbish.

The of Gilipoli was inhabited chiefly by Greeks and
Bulgarians, with a few Armenians, and Turks, who traded
in different branches, some in the public Sale of Liquors
others dealt in Groceries, others in Butter, Eggs, Milk
Sweetmeats and different other articles and they appeared
to be driving a good Trade. At the time the British
Army was Marching through their Country on their way
to the Crimea.

About noon on the 17th of May we left Galipoli and
proceeded on our way towards the Ground we were
to Encamp on, There was a portion of the French
Army Encamped about two miles from the Town of
Galipoli, and when our Column came up to their
camp they turned out of their Tents and gave us
a hearty cheer, and Numbers of the Men came over
to our ranks and shook hands with us, and procured

lights for our Pipes, and gave us what we were much
in need of, good Water which much refreshed us
and they did it with seeming kindness and good
nature, considering that this was the first time
that England and France Met together as
Brothers in Arms.

After a tedious and Fatigueing March through
Mud and Mire, and over uneven Roads, we
came to the Ground we were to Encamp upon,
we there Pitched of our heavy Knapsacks on the
ground, piled our Arms, took off our Accoutrements
And began to prepare the ground for Pitching our
Tents, that being done and our Sentries placed
on their posts for the Safety of all our Troops,
we sat down to get a little Refreshment after
the Fatigue of the day, Nor was it long ere the
floors of our Tents were covered with Bread,
Butter, Eggs, and plenty of good Wine, both
white and Red, for 4ᵈ per quart, And as this
was the first time of our being on the Turkish soil
we were determined to make ourselves as comfortable
as circumstances would permit, and there being
an Abundance of good wine at hand we did
not fail to do so, After drinking to the health
of our Wives, and Sweethearts, and our Friends
at home, And offering up a Prayer to the Throne
of Mercy, for success against our Foes. we
through ourselves down upon our beds of Clay
and slept like Warriors untill Aroused by the
Drums beating to Arms at daylight the following
Morning, We remained there for a short time,
during the time we was there the Sun was very
hott, and unhealthy,

We then received an Order to proceed to Balshac
to relieve the 4ᵗʰ 28ᵗʰ and 44, Regiments who were
employed there in constructing Batteries and
throwing up Earthworks as a protection against

the Enemy if needed, which opperations we comme
after arriving there. Our Chief Employment during
our stay there was in erecting Wooden Barrack
to serve as a Winter Quarters if required, but
we were not destined to remain there there to,
as we were alloted for more active Service, and
after a short stay in Bullahar, we received Order
to join the Grand Army under the Command of
Lord Raglan, then Stationed in Varna
On the 28th of June in the same year we
Marched from Bullahar to Galipili and Embarked
on Board, H. M. T. Ship Golden Fleece, and
proceeded on our way to Varna, On the way to
the above named place we passed that Celibrated
place Constantinople, It was a beautiful
morning in June, when we first came in
sight of it It Nealy was a beautiful sight
to us who saw it for the first time, there was
the Grand Palace of the Sultans and ajoining it
was the Sareglao de Harem where he keeps his
365 Wifes With Mosques, Cathedrals, and other
places of Worship of all shapes and Sizes, and
these Veiwed from the River as we sailed gently
along, afforded one of most pleasing sights that
any eye could behold, We stayed in the Habor
about one Hour to leave a few Men at Scutaria
who were sick, and during that short stay
the Vessel was surrounded by the inhabitants
with Bum Boats, Filled with all kinds of
Fruit, Sweetmeats, and other Articles pleasing to
the eye, and Suitable to the Pallat, there was
the rich Grape, Beautiful Peaches, Apricots,
Oranges, Lemons, Apples, Nuts, Figs, in fact
every thing that could tempt the beholder to
purchase

After delivering our sick Men into the hands of
the Medical Officers, Stationed there We then
proceeded on our way to Varna and as we passed
through the Bosphorus the scene was lovely in
extreem around us, and as we was close to
land all the way up we enjoyed it very
much

We arrived in Varna on the 26th of June in the
Evening and disembarked about 9 OClock the
following Morning, were we were met by a great
Number of our Comrade Soldiers, who welcomed
us cheerfully, knowing we had come to take
an active part in Meals that awaited us in
the East

We Encamped near the Shumla Road about
three miles from the Town of Varna, at this
place the Army was told off into 5 Divisions
each Division Numbering about 5,000 Men
not including Cavalry, Artillery On Royal
Engineers which numbered about 3,000 More
Men.   We had not been in Varna more then
a Month when we were Reviewed by the Allied
Commanders, On the Plains of Bulgaria who
expressed themselves highly satisfied with our
Soldier like appearance, and the perfect state
of discipline, And they could say that without
Flattery, for a finer Body of Men never
left the Shoes of Old England, then was
assembled on those Plains that day, Men who
were able and willing to meet any equal force
in the world

During our stay at Varna we were employed
daily in making roads for the conveyence of
our Commissariat stores and Field Equipage
from the Harbour to the Camp

as the Turks never thought of doing any thing of the kind themselves, nor would they assist us unless compelled to do so, which means we often had to resort to, as they were the most lazy and dirty set of people (you may call them savages) in the world and not worth fighting for, however we managed to change the appearance of them altogether before we left it

At this time the Month of June was past and July come in, and it was most intensely hot, the Sun is Pouring its most Powerful Heat upon us the whole day long while we we at work from daylight in the Morning untill dark at night in removeing our stores and Field Equipage such as shot, shell, powder, Grape, Rockets, and everything necessary for a Campaign

About the Tenth day of this Month the camp was completely darkened with a swarm of Locusts, it was about 8 OClock in the Evening that the approach of them was first noticed by a buzzing that much resembled a gail of wind. So great was their Number that they Destroyed the Vines for Miles round as they passed through the country, they did not fly more then 14 or 15 feet from the ground and the Inhabitants told us that there coming was a sure sign of sickness prevailing amongst us and to our regret we found their statement to be correct for in the course of a week after we lost sight of them, there was a dreadfull disease of that fatal Cholrea raging through our Camps which caused a great Havock through our

ranks, Only you would think all the men were paralized
Hundreds of our best men were taken off by it, in Life
then a week from the time it made its first
appearance amongst us, At that time there used
generaly to sleep in each Tent from ten to twelve
Men, And considering the small space each man
occupied which was only 21 inches in Breadth
that together with the intence heat of the weather
made the Tents at night when the Allotted
Number were inside, Almost insupportable I
have seen three or four Comrade Soldiers
who lay down at night to rest from the heavy
Fatigues they had gone through during the day
As well in health as they were the day they left
the Land of their Birth, Rehearsing to each
other the different incidents they had witnessed
through the day, And a good merry song would
accompany it untill they would all fall
fast asleep when everything for a time was
forgotten, And then perhaps at the dead of
the night they would be called upon to call
the Docter to the Tent or assist in taking
the man to Hospital for when once it caught
hold of a man it was great misery, not
one alone but perhaps two or three at the
same time, their limbs stiffening in Death
and their Features soon changed with the
Agonizing Pain that racked their Frames
Yet it was scarsely worth while taking
them to Hospital for when this dreadfull
desease once got hold of the frame the Grave
was his doom there was No Alternative, no cure,
nor release from the dreadful pains that were
Racking his frame untill death stepped in
and put an end to his sufferings, such
dreadful scenes of this discription have I
witnessed that would almost freeze the blood

on mes Veins, and those poor fellows who were Thousands of miles from their Country and Friends, lying upon a bed of clay and Death when no tender Mother, or Kind Father, were there, to administer to his wants or to sooth him in his sufferings, What a contrast between the Death bed of a Soldier in a far off Clime, and the one at home, the one at home is surrounded by kind Friends, and Relations, Perhaps Father, Mother, Brothers, and Sisters, all are there administering to him as much as possible all his wants soothing, and comforting him in his last departing moments while the poor Crimean Soldier experienced none of these attendants, No not one, God grant that we may never witness such scenes as I did during my stay in Turkey

We have now got into the Month of August when another callamity, though of another description which caused us to stay longer in Turkey than we otherwise should have done What occasioned this, was, an alarming Fire that broke out in our stores situated in the Town of Varna

On the 10th of August of the same year and about 8 OClock in the Evening the Allied Camps were suddenly Alarmed by the Cry of fire the Troops were instantly Ordered to proceed at once to the scene of Conflagration which at this time could ~~at this time~~ be seen for Miles round the place The first place

the fire broke out was at our Commissariat
Stores but how it originated is not known the
Stores were filled with provisions of all kinds
Such as Biscuit, Beef, Pork, Rum, Sugar, Tea,
Coffee, and other Articles for the use of the Troops
in abundance, And the ajoining Bilding to
this was our Main Magazine filled with
Powder, Live Shell, Rocketts, Shott, and
other Combustibles for Siege opperations and
had that Building caught fire it would
have blown all the Town and what it
contained to attoms but fortuneately it
escaped With prompt assistance being
Rendered by the Allied Powers Every thing
was soon placed out of the way of the Flames
and in safely, And when we had done so we
all began to solace ourselves with a cup of
good Brandy or Wine, as it was running
down the Streets in Hogsheads of which the
Troops, Both English and French partook of
freely, The fire was not properly estinguished
for nearly a week, during which time we were
employed in getting our stores on Board a
Ship, Preparity to our leaving Varna, that
British Grave Yard for such it has proved
to hundreds of Brave English Men
At this time we have everything in readiness
to leave this fatal place of decease and
Death, But before quitting it I will
endeavour to give a faint Idea of the
Customs and Manners of the Inhabitants
I will first begin with Jona Bono
himself, they are dirty, Lazy, slothful,
and wretched Savages —
The Mans dress is as follows his head is

covered with a kind of rough Furze Cap, such
as I never saw in England or Ireland and as
regards the make or shape of it and the way it
is worn exceeds any thing I ever saw
There is then several yards of cotton cloth wound
round closely to the head what is called in
that Country a Turban
Next is, there is no hair on there head only
a small tuft just on the Crown its something
like a cat tail they are under the opinion
that they will be drawn up to Heaven
by that when they die —
Next comes the coat or jacket its of a very
rough kind of sacken Varigated all over
with different coulered lace or Braid something
like a Merry — Mans in a Pantomime on
the stage of some Theatre with the sleeves
hanging useless by their shoulders.
Next what the term Cacklimonies they are
made something after the manner of an English
Womans Peticoat, tying round the waist
with a strong cord, and sewed at the bottom
leaving a small hole at the two corners to
pass there two feet and legs through it
then reaches to there knees —
Next the Feet they cut a piece of Horse
or Buffelo hide to the shape of the foot
cut small holes all around it piece and
with a thong of the same Material it
is drawn tight to the Ancle there whole
Breast and legs are exposed to the intense
heat of that unhealthy Climate
Now for that fair set the Woman —

SUGGESTIONS FOR FURTHER READING

Royle, Trevor - *Crimea: The Great Crimean War 1854-1856* - Abacus, 2000.

Hope, Robert - *A Staffordshire Regiment in the Crimea: 38th Regiment of Foot* - Churnet Valley Books, 2003.

Vane, W L - *The Durham Light Infantry* - Gale & Polden, 1914.

Carter, Thomas - *Historical Record of the Forty-Fourth* - W. O. Mitchell, 1864

The Crimean War Research Society website, *http://cwrs.russianwar.co.uk,* provides access to a wide range of resources.

ACKNOWLEDGEMENTS

I would like to thank the following, without whose assistance it is unlikely Richard Barnham's journal would have been published at this time:

Jeff Elson, Head of Research at the Staffordshire Regiment Museum in Litchfield, who helped me rediscover the 'long-lost' journal.
http://staffordshireregimentmuseum.com

David Cliff, Founder & Vice-President of the Crimean War Research Society, who took the time to read the journal and write an exciting and insightful foreword.
http://cwrs.russianwar.co.uk

The Ancestry Information Operations Company, whose website, *http://ancestry.co.uk*, provided many of the dates and most of the background information on Richard Barnham's life.

Marion Russell, my grandma, who first provided me with a copy of this journal.

If you have enjoyed this book, please consider reviewing it on Amazon or Goodreads (or both)

And feel free visit the Lundarien Press website for other titles and to view the original journal pages:

WWW.LUNDARIENPRESS.COM

28103564R00077

Printed in Great Britain
by Amazon